SKILL BUILDING FOR ESL AND SPECIAL EDUCATION

SIMPLY ENGLISH SERIES

Simply English is an ESL curriculum adaptable for elementary though adult learners. Its goal is to help the limited and/or non-English speaker achieve fluency in English words that are essential for everyday life. Simply English can also be incorporated into special education programs for students who need help with spelling, definitions of words, and correct application of grammatical structures. The forty-four instructional units contain the basic information that ELS and special education students need to function independently.

Books in the Series:

Skill Building for ESL and Special Education: Teacher's Text
Skill Building for ESL and Special Education: Student Workbook
Skill Building for ESL and Special Education: Student Textbook

IILDING FOR ESL
CIAL EDUCATION

Student Textbook

Kristine Setting Clark

Rowman & Littlefield
Lanham • Boulder • New York • London

Published by Rowman & Littlefield
A wholly owned subsidiary of The Rowman & Littlefield Publishing Group, Inc.
4501 Forbes Boulevard, Suite 200, Lanham, Maryland 20706
www.rowman.com

Unit A, Whitacre Mews, 26-34 Stannary Street, London SE11 4AB

British Library Cataloguing in Publication Information Available

Library of Congress Cataloging-in-Publication Data Available

978-1-4758-2633-3 (paper)
978-1-4758-2634-0 (electronic)

∞™ The paper used in this publication meets the minimum requirements of American
National Standard for Information Sciences—Permanence of Paper for Printed Library
Materials, ANSI/NISO Z39.48-1992.

Printed in the United States of America

Contents

Introduction

The *Simply English Textbook* will help you to achieve fluency in English words and phrases which are essential for everyday life. There is also a coordinating *Simply English Workbook* to be used along with the textbook to give you practice with spelling, word definitions, and correct application of grammatical structures.

The forty-four units are organized, presented, and applied to everyday, real-life situations. They include whole class and small group activities. Each unit contains the following material:

Competency Goals

Vocabulary: Listen, Read, Say

Structures and Skill Building

The advantage of this *topical approach* to learning English is that it can be expanded or revised according to your academic or social interests and needs. The units are not to be considered sequential; therefore, they may be used in whichever order is suitable for the class. The primary purpose of this approach is to develop *immediately* usable oral and written communication skills. These units are situation-oriented and *minimally structured*. They should not be considered solely as grammar lessons.

I have been using this material with my students and the results have been fantastic! Their comprehension and practical use of the English language have been beyond my greatest expectations. My main reason for writing *Simply English* is that although there has been a lot of material written for English as a second language (ESL) and special education, there was nothing that seemed suitable for everyday use.

Simply English is a new approach to teaching and learning—different from the traditional style. You now have the opportunity to practice skills in reading, writing, listening, and speaking. You will also develop confidence in self-expression.

I hope you will find *Simply English* a refreshing and easy approach for your efforts to learn English. I am sure you will find the results to be extremely rewarding.

1

Personal Identification I

Competency Goals

To be able to self-identify.

To be able to give address, phone number, city, and state.

To be able to give and respond to a simple greeting.

To be able to introduce and tell something about another student in the class.

To be able to open, continue, and close a conversation in both formal and informal situations.

Vocabulary: Listen, Read, Say

introduction	good-bye	our	nationality/ethnicity
to introduce	bye	my	nation
to meet	see you later	friend	United States
I'd like	what's	father	U.S.A.
hello	it's	mother	weekend
hi	she's	sister	days of the week
pleased	he's	brother	Monday
pleasure	they're	teacher	Tuesday
glad	we're	formal language	Wednesday
Mr.	your	informal language	Thursday
Mrs.	his	greeting	Friday
Miss	her	to leave	Saturday
Ms.	their	to say good-bye	Sunday

Structures and Skill Building: Introductions—Formal Language

Maria, this is _____.	I (he, she, they, you) came to the United States by _____.
I'd like to introduce _____.	I'm (he's, she's, they're, we're) from _____.
Maria, I'd like you to meet _____.	What are our (their) names?
Mrs. Lee, this is _____.	What's his (her, you're, my) name?
I'm very glad to meet you.	Yes, it is.
How do you do?	No, it isn't.
Nice to meet you.	Yes, they are.
Pleased to meet you.	No, they aren't.
It's a pleasure to meet you.	
Hello.	
Hi.	
This is my (your, his, her, their, our) friend (mother, father, brother, teacher) _____.	

Opening Conversations—Formal Language

Opening conversations can begin with the subjects listed below or you can make up subjects of your own.

Your state

Your city

Your school

ELS class or other classes

Changing classes

The weather

I like/don't like (city, state, class, etc.) very much. _____ is (very, really) different from _____.

Opening, Continuing, and Closing Conversations—Informal Language

You will quickly be exposed to the American "slang" that is commonly spoken in the United States. These informal expressions can be expanded upon if so desired.

How are you?	How are you doing?
Fine	Good.
OK	Not bad.
Thanks.	Thank you.
And you?	How about you?
Did you have a nice/good weekend?	How was your weekend?
Well, bye/good-bye.	Bye.
See you (day/time).	See you.
See you later.	Later.
Have a good (nice) day/weekend.	Have a good one.

2

Personal Identification II

Competency Goals

To be able to give more extensive information about themselves and seek the same from others.

To be able to fill out school forms.

To be able to identify cardinal and ordinal numbers.

To be able to recite the days of the week, months of the year, and the seasons.

Vocabulary: Listen, Read, Say

to sign	registration form	birth
print	attending	birthday/birthdate
signature	immunization(s)	grade/year in school
first name	inoculation(s)	address
last name	vaccination(s)	street
middle name/initial	shots	avenue
citizen/citizenship	allergies	boulevard
passport	bleeder	road
green card/visa	physical disabilities	drive
nationality	doctor	court
sex	hospital	area code/telephone number
male	emergency	
female	notify	
boy	information	city
girl	born	state
man	weight	zip code
woman	height	county
	parent's name	country/native country

business address	guardian's name	
business phone		
military	cardinal numbers (one, two, three)	
health plan #	ordinal numbers (first, second, third)	
talk/speak	zero	
languages	days of the week	
calendar	weekend	
schedule/courses/classes	months and seasons	

Structures and Skill Building

What's your name (address, phone number, city, state, zip code, county)?

Where were you born? What is your place of birth/birthplace?

What is your date of birth/birthday/birthdate? How old are you?

Where are you from? What is your country of citizenship?

How long have you been or lived in this country?

In case of emergency notify (name, address, and/or phone number).

Please sign (write, print) your name here.

Please sign (write, print) your name on this line.

We must have/need your signature.

What language do you (we, they) speak?

What language is spoken at home?

3

Education and Schooling I

Competency Goals

To be able to give information about yourself and seek the same from others with regard to your school and schedule.

To know other teachers' names.

To understand school procedures.

To understand general school terminology.

Vocabulary: Listen, Read, Say

grade(s) 6th, 7th, 8th, 9th, 10th, 11th, 12th	mandatory
sixth, seventh, eighth, ninth, tenth	elective courses
eleventh, twelfth	grades/report card
elementary school/grade school	quarter/semester
middle school	class schedule
junior high school	courses/classes/electives
high school	period(s)
previous school	session(s)
school name	homework
school address	break
city and state	lunch
zip code	referral/detention/suspension
phone number	tardy
email address/website	inappropriate behavior
	hall pass
English/ESL/Language Arts	re-admit slip
Math	off-campus permit

Physical education / PE / gym	
Computer Technology	homework
History / Social Studies / Civics	teacher / teachers' names
Science / Physical / Life	to attend school / class(es)
Music	to go to school / class(es)
Art	minimum day / schedule change
Business	minimum day schedule
World Language	holiday / vacation / break
Drama / Theater	fire drill
Career Technology	assembly
	elections

Structures and Skill Building

What was her (his, your, their) previous school grade?	What school did you (he, she, they, we) attend (go to) last year?
My (her, his, our, their) previous school / grade was _____.	I (he, she, they, we) attended (went to) _____ last year.
What grade were you (we, they) in last year?	We (You, They) were in _____ grade last year.
What grade was she (he) in last year?	She (He) was in _____ grade last year.
I'm (He's, She's, They're, We're, You're) in (the) _____ grade this year.	What classes / courses is he (she) taking?
What's his (her, your, their) schedule?	What classes / courses are you (they) taking?
What school does he (she) attend / go to?	What school do you (they) attend / go to?
What school is he (she) attending?	What school are you (they) attending?
What's the school / school's address?	

What's the school/school's phone number?	
What's the school/school's email address/ website?	
What are your teachers' names?	
What classes did you take last year/last semester?	
What were your teachers' names?	

4

Education and Schooling II

Competency Goals

To be able to give information about yourself and seek information from others in regard to school buildings and rooms.

To know the names and titles of school personnel.

To be able to identify and correctly spell classroom equipment.

To be able to correctly respond to verbal and written commands.

Vocabulary: Listen, Read, Say

Buildings, Room, and Related Items

business office	eraser
attendance office	pen
counselor's office	paper
library	ruler
restroom/bathroom	iPad/binder/notebook/laptop/tablet
classroom	backpack/book bag
multipurpose room/auditorium	blackboard/chalkboard/white board/dry board
gymnasium	chalk/markers
computer lab	seat/chair
science lab	desk
cafeteria	row
locker room/PE locker	table
book locker	stapler/staples/staple remover
combination lock	tape
pencil/pencil sharpener	paper clip(s)

School Personnel

principal	para/paraprofessional
assistant principal	aide/volunteer
counselor	yard duty
librarian	campus supervisor
custodian	school police/campus security
teacher	secretary
nurse	school psychiatrist/psychologist

School Equipment

posters	copy machine/scanner/fax
flag	DVD/CD
map	computer
TV/television	glue/paste/tape
file cabinet	clock
bookcase/bookcases	calendar
shelf/shelves	
podium	

Related Terminology

right/left	to memorize
near, next to, behind	to add a class
in front of, above, below	to drop a class
before, during, after	to change your schedule
time/time of day	
first through seventh period	requirement(s)
semester	credits/units
quarter	graduation/graduate
to lecture	to graduate
to take notes	to promote/promotion
to teach	proofread
to take a course	rough draft/rewrite
to study	final copy
study habits	
to pass	
to fail	

Commands

to pledge allegiance	to head your paper
to borrow/to lend	to exchange
to turn on/to turn off	to correct
to go to	to put (in, on, under, etc.)
to return to	to copy
to sit	to write
to stand	to listen
to sharpen	to write down a homework assignment
to pass (up, back, out, etc.)	to follow directions
to erase	

Structures and Skill Building

Where's the (name of building/room)?

Where is (room #)?

The (name of building/room) is next (near, behind, etc.) to (name of building).

How do I (you, we, they) get to (room #)?

You (We, They) (give directions how to get there).

May I borrow a (an, some) _____?

Sure.

I'm sorry, I didn't have a (an, any) _____.

Turn on/off (name of equipment).

Sit at _____.

Sharpen your pencil.

Erase your errors on (the board).

Staple _____.

Exchange _____.

Pass up _____.

Correct _____.

Write down your homework assignment for tonight.

Copy the directions on the board.

Head your paper.

Return to your set/desk.

Stand for the Pledge of Allegiance.

Go to the _____.

What time is it?

The time is _____.

When do you have (name of class)?

It's _____ period.

I need to add/drop a class.

I want to change my schedule.

What are the requirements for graduation?

How many credits/units do I need to graduate?

I have _____ credits/units.

You need _____ credits/units to graduate.

5

The Telephone/The Cell Phone

Competency Goals

To be able to give information about yourself and seek information from others with regard to the telephone and its use.

To understand the use of the phone book and the Internet's white and yellow pages.

To be able to make long distance, collect, and emergency calls.

To be able to converse over the phone in English with others (e.g., friends, family, business).

To be able to understand the many features and apps (applications) of a cell phone.

Vocabulary: Listen, Read, Say

to telephone/to phone	wrong number
to call	disconnected
to make a call	no longer in service
to leave a message	unlisted number
to take a message	
to wait	public telephone
to hear	telephone operator
to be cut off/dropped call	overseas operator
to hang up	
	long distance call
to make a long distance call	local call
to use the operator	emergency call (911)
to receive a call	"crank" call
to return a call	toll-free number (800, 888, etc.)

hello	cell phone
please	smartphone
thank you	importing and creating contacts
May I ask who's calling?	making and receiving calls
May I take a message?	dead zones / dropped calls
The line is busy.	text messaging: sending / receiving / forwarding / saving
good-bye	email: sending / receiving / forwarding / saving
telephone service / telephone provider (e.g., Verizon, AT&T, Sprint)	Web browsing: Opening links, bookmarks, GPS (Global Positioning System) features
telephone bill	photo taking / video recording
telephone plan	editing
unlimited minutes / text / data	sharing photos / videos / web pages / files
	personalization: setting wall papers / ringtones / vibration patterns / brightness / do not disturb
cordless phone	security: setting a lock / screen name / screen password / securing and back up for your contacts and applications / securing your personal information
answering machine	organization: organizing your home screen / music / photos and videos
phone / fax machine	
	app (application) store: downloading and using apps / free apps / paid apps
telephone cord	
dial tone	data
automatic redial	
call waiting	
conference call	
mute button	
receiver	
blocked call	
telephone directory / book	
yellow pages / white pages	
telephone numbers / contacts	

Structures and Skill Building

How many telephones/phones are there in your home?

There are _____ telephones/phones in my home.

Do you use the phone a lot?

Yes, I use the phone/it a lot.

No, I don't use the phone/it a lot.

Who do you call the most?

I call _____ the most. (Tell how often).

Do you have a cell phone? What kind?

Yes, I have a/an (kind of phone).

No, I don't have a cell phone.

Can you take pictures/videos on your phone?

Yes, I can take pictures/videos on my phone.

No, I can't take pictures/videos on my phone.

How many contacts do you have on your phone?

I have (amount) contacts on my phone.

Do you have email on your phone?

Yes, I have email on my phone.

No, I don't have email on my phone.

What kind of phone plan do you have? Who is your provider?

I have a/an limited/unlimited plan. My provider is _____.

Do you ever call your native country? How much is it to call your native country?

Yes, I call (name of native country). It costs (amount) to call my native country.

No, I don't call (name of native country).

6

Behavior

Competency Goals

To be able to give information about yourself and seek information from others with regard to appropriate and inappropriate behavior.

To know the difference between acceptable and unacceptable behavior in the United States in comparison to other countries.

To know when to use the phrases *Please, Thank you, I'm sorry,* and *Excuse me.*

To be able to write invitations and thank-you notes.

Vocabulary: Listen, Read, Say

polite/courteous behavior	impolite/discourteous behavior
appropriate behavior	inappropriate behavior
correct	incorrect
right	wrong
approved	unapproved
acceptable	unacceptable
manners	requests (asking for something)
courtesy/courteous	invitations (inviting someone)
interrupt, interruption	offer/offering (willing to give)
forgive/forgiveness	thank-you note
apologize, apology	get-well card
please	sympathy card (to sympathize)
thank you	RSVP (please respond/reply)
I'm sorry	
excuse me/pardon me	complain/complaining
cultural differences	compliment/complimenting
eye contact (with adults as well as children)	covering your mouth when you: yawn, sneeze, cough, laugh

Structures and Skill Building

Using "Please" and "Thank you" to get someone to do something for you or to give something to you

Could you please move over one seat?	Sure.
Thanks a lot.	
Could you please loan me a pen?	Sorry, I don't have an extra one.
Thanks, anyway.	
Could I please have change for a dollar?	Sure. How would you like it?
I'd like three quarters, two dimes, and a nickel, please.	Here you are.
Thanks.	

Using "Excuse me" and "Pardon me"

Excuse me. Do you have the time?	Sure. It's 5:00.
Thanks.	
Pardon me. Could you tell me how to get to Abraham Lincoln High School?	Sure. Go two blocks west on Quintara Street. Then turn left on 25th Avenue. It's on your left.
Thank you very much.	

Inviting and Offering

I'm having a party next Saturday night. Would you like to come?	Sure.
Great! I'll give you the details later.	Thanks.
Would you like to go to the movies Friday night?	I'm sorry but I'm busy.
Maybe next time.	Yeah. Thanks anyway.
May I help you with your coat?	Yes, thanks.

Apologizing

Please turn down your TV. It's too loud.	Oh, I'm sorry. I didn't realize it was so loud.

| Gee, I'm really sorry I broke your pen. | Oh, that's OK. I've got another one. |
| Well, I'll buy you another one anyway. | Thanks. |

Offering Condolences

| I'm sorry to hear about you brother's accident. How is he? | He's OK, thanks. The doctor says he'll be back to school in about a week or so. |
| Great! I'll try to get by and see him soon. | Oh, that would be nice. He'd like that very much. |

Writing and Sending 'Thank-you' notes for presents, invitations, etc.

Date_____

Dear _____

_____

_____

_____

_____

_____

_____

_____

_____

Signature _____

7

Family Relationships

Competency Goals

To be able to give and seek information regarding family relationships.

To be able to identify family members and relations.

To be able to plan out and chart a family tree.

Vocabulary: Listen, Read, Say

Male	Female	Both Sexes
husband	wife	spouse/partner
father	mother	parent
brother	sister	sibling
son	daughter	child
grandson	granddaughter	grandchild
grandfather	grandmother	grandparent
great-grandfather	great-grandmother	great-grandparent
uncle	aunt	
nephew	niece	
stepfather	stepmother	stepparent
stepson	stepdaughter	stepchild
half brother	half sister	
godfather	godmother	godparent
godson	goddaughter	godchild
bachelor	bachelorette	
divorce	divorcee	
widower	widow	
father-in-law	mother-in-law	in-law

son-in-law	daughter-in-law	
brother-in-law	sister-in-law	
man/men	woman/women	adult
boy	girl	child/children
		baby/babies
		adolescent
		teenager
		youth
		young person/people

Related Terminology

married	generation
single	ancestors
separated	family tree
divorced	adopted/adoption
companion	relative(s)
nickname(s)	foster parents
maiden name	foster child
twins/triplets/multiple births	custody
cousin(s)	extended family
dysfunctional family	

Structures and Skill Building

Do you have a (name of family member)?	Yes, I have (#)_____ member(s).
Do you have any (name of family member)?	No, I don't have a/any (member(s)).
How old is your (name of family member)?	My _____ is _____ (years old).
How old are your (name of family member)?	My _____are _____ (years old).
	My _____ is _____ and my _____ is _____.

	He/She is _____ (years old).
	They are _____ and _____ (years old).
Do you have an older/a younger brother or sister?	Yes, I have an older/a younger _____.
	No, I don't have an older/a younger _____.
I'm married.	
He's single.	
She's widowed.	
They're divorced.	
We're separated.	
You're adopted.	

8

Occupations

Competency Goals

To be able to give and seek information about various occupations.

To be able to discuss various occupations and what they entail.

To be able to discuss and/or write about the occupation most appealing to you.

Vocabulary: Listen, Read, Say

student (full time/part time)	dry cleaner
farmer/farm worker	photographer
employee	plumber
office worker	guard/watchman
receptionist	beautician/hairdresser/barber
secretary/assistant	broadcaster/announcer
teacher/instructor/professor	disk jockey/DJ
aide	author/writer
businessman/businesswoman	bus driver
executive/manager/management	taxi driver
judge	truck driver
lawyer/attorney	chef/cook/baker
doctor/surgeon/specialist	short order cook
nurse	waiter/waitress/bartender
paramedic	dishwasher
druggist/pharmacist	athlete
dentist/orthodontist/specialist	policeman/woman
dental technician/hygienist	firefighter
veterinarian	banker/bank teller

milkman	accountant
deliveryman	broker
paperboy/papergirl	butcher
computer technician/computer repair	salesman/saleswoman
custodian	soldier
gardener/landscaper	sailor
painter	pilot
carpenter	flight attendant
construction worker	stewardess/steward
engineer	florist
architect	repairman
electrician	babysitter
mechanic	mail carrier/postman/woman
actor/actress/TV personality	postal worker
singer/dancer	social worker
comedian	telephone operator
clown	dietician/nutritionist
clerk	housewife
cashier/checker	housekeeper/maid
busboy/girl	porter
bellhop/redcap	longshoreman
musician	miner
journalist/reporter	model

Related Terminology

job	unemployed
occupation	employer/employee
profession	firm
career	company
to do for a living	supervisor/boss/foreman/manager
to work	food stamps
to have a job/to be employed	job fair
to be on welfare	help wanted
Aid to Families with Dependent Children	to look for a job

Structures and Skill Building

What do you do?

What do you do for a living?

What does your father (mother, sister, brother, etc.) do for a living?

What is your (his, her, their, our) occupation?

What is your (his, her, their, our) job?

I'm a/an _____.

I am a/an _____ at _____.

He (She) is a/an _____.

He (She) is a/an _____ at _____.

You (They) are _____.

Where does your (name of relative) work?

He (She) works at/in _____.

Where do you work?

I don't work. I don't work because I'm a full-time student.

I work at _____. I work at _____ in _____.

Do you have a job?

Yes, I do. I'm a _____ at/in _____.

No, I don't. I'm a full-time student.

Did you ever work?

No, I didn't.

Have you ever worked?

No, I haven't.

Yes, I worked at (place) (when).

Yes, I worked as (a, an) (job) at (place) (when).

9

Health I

Parts of the Body

Competency Goals

To be able to give information about yourself and seek information from others with regard to parts of your body.

To know where all body parts are located—inside and outside the body.

Vocabulary: Listen Read, Say

Parts of the Body

head	lips	stomach	leg
brain	jaw	waist	thigh
hair	tooth/teeth	hips	knee
face	gums	arm	shin
eyes	tongue	shoulder	calf
eyelids	throat	elbow	foot
eyebrows	cheek	wrist	ankle
eyelashes	mustache	hand	heel
ears	beard	palm	toes
mouth	chest	fingers	toenails
nose	heart	fingernails	back
sinuses	lungs	knuckle	spine
skin	breast	thumb	spinal cord
forehead		muscle(s)	vertebrae
		bones	vertebrae column

Related Terminology

on top of	above
below	under
next to	to attach/detach
to insert	origin and insertion of muscles

How many (body part) do we/you/they have?

We/you/they have (#) (body part).

How many (body part) does he/she/everybody have?

He/She/Everybody has (#) (body part).

Does he/she/everybody have a/an (body part)?

Yes, he/she/everybody has a/an (body part).

No, you/we/they don't have a/an (body part).

Do you/we/they have a/an (body part)?

Yes, you/we/they have a/an (body part).

No, you/we/they don't have a/an (body part).

Where is your (body part)?

My (body part) is located (show or explain where).

10

Health II

Ailments and Accidents

Competency Goals

To be able to give information about yourself and seek information from others with regard to ailments and accidents.

To be able to describe symptoms of certain illnesses.

To know how to react/respond to any given situation involving sickness and/or accident.

Vocabulary: Listen, Read, Say

Ailments	Accidents
headache	to fall
earache	to break
toothache	to twist
stomachache	to sprain
cramps/pains	to cut/to puncture
chills	to trip
fever/temperature	to slip
injury/wound	to skin
scratch	to bleed
cut/puncture	to bruise
sore	
blister	
infection	
cold	
cough	
sore throat	
laryngitis	

bleeder/bleeding	
allergies	
sore, itchy, scratchy eyes	
stuffy nose	
hay fever	
twisted/sprained/pulled body part	
bruised/broken body part	
bruise	

Related Terminology

What's the matter?	to feel . . .	operation/surgery/procedure
to hurt	dizzy	health/healthy
to happen	ache/achy all over	inside/outside
to move	faint/pass out	to use/treat
to stabilize	very weak	bandage/band aid
to need	nauseous	ointment
to sleep	awful	stitches
to drink	run-down	cast
to throw up/vomit	sick/ill	sling
to go to the bathroom	sleepy	crutches/brace(s)
to lower/raise	tired	wheelchair
to elevate	thirsty	
cause(s)	hungry	medical insurance
symptom(s)	better	
remedy/remedies	worse	
to take medicine/medication/ meds	comfortable	

Structures and Skill Building

How do you feel?

I feel sick.

I don't feel well.

He/She feels sick.

He/She doesn't feel well.

What hurts?

My (body part) hurts.

Where does it hurt?

It hurts here (point to body part).

Does it hurt inside or outside?

It hurts (inside or outside).

Can you tell me what hurts?

I have a (description of ailment).

Can you tell me where it hurts?

I (use one of the accident verbs) my (body part).

I can't move my (body part).

He/She has a/an (description of ailment)

He/She (accident verb) his/her (body part).

He/She can't move his/her (body part).

What happened?

I (He/She) had a bad accident (when).

I (He/She) (description of accident).

What do you need?

I need a bandage for my (body part).

He/She needs a bandage for his/her (body part).

May I see the nurse, please?

What do you want to do?

I think I have to (should) go home.

I feel (awful, sick, nauseous, etc.).

I have the/a/an (ailment).

How's your father (mother, brother, sister, etc.) been?

He's/She's (description).

Tell him/her I hope he's/she's feeling better soon.

Thanks, I will.

11

Health III

The Doctor/The Hospital

Competency Goals

To be able to give information about yourself and seek information about others with regard to doctor and hospital services.

To be able to locate phone numbers of local doctors, hospitals, ambulance, and paramedic services.

To be able to make a doctor's appointment.

To be able to describe an accident requiring medical attention.

Vocabulary: Listen, Read, Say

to get sick	to suffer
to become ill	to live
to take your pulse	to die
to take your temperature	to recover
to take your blood pressure	to listen/to listen to
to operate/to need surgery	to make an appointment
to bandage	to get a physical/medical exam
doctor's office	sickness/illness
waiting room	grave/serious
nurse	disease
patient	virus
doctor/physician	infection
surgeon	incubation/incubation period
specialist	chicken pox
first aid	measles/German measles
private room	mumps
semiprivate room	influenza/flu

ward	tonsils/tonsillectomy
visiting hours	appendix/appendectomy
visitor	inoculation/shot/injection
appointment/appointment card	preventative medicine/screening
operation/surgery/procedure	immunization/vaccination
hospital/emergency room	blood test/sample
urine sample	
main entrance	stethoscope
outpatient	heartbeat/heart rate
admitting	blood pressure
reception desk	flashlight
administration	tongue depressor
insurance/medical coverage	thermometer
ambulance/paramedic(s)	x-ray/CAT scan/MRI/EKG
operating room	wheelchair
examining table	crutches
hospital gown	sling/splint/cast
triage	maternity ward
recovery room	intensive care unit (ICU)
coma/comatose	
to get a check-up	

Structures and Skill Building

I don't feel well.

If you don't feel well, go to/call the doctor/hospital.

What seems to be the problem/trouble?

Do you have a (state the problem)?

It sounds like you have a (problem).

It's probably a (problem).

I need/have to see a doctor.

I need/have to see Dr. _____.

Make an appointment.

Hello. I need an appointment with Dr. _____.

What seems to be the problem/trouble?

I (description of problem).

Can you come in (day) at (time)?

Yes. I'll write it down.

Please repeat the time.

(Day) and (time).

Thank you.

You're welcome. See you then.

At the Emergency Room

I (He, She, We) (description of problem).

We'll need some information.

Please fill out this form.

The doctor will be right with you.

Calling an Ambulance/Paramedics

I need an ambulance (a paramedic) right away for _____.

Where do you live?

My address is _____.

My mother (father, sister, brother, etc.) (description of problem).

How old is _____?

How is his/her breathing?

How is his/her skin color?

Is he/she hot or cold? Or, what is his/her temperature/body temperature?

12

Health IV

The Drugstore

Competency Goals

To be able to give information about yourself and seek information from others with regard to prescription drugs, nonprescription, drugs, and other related health products.

To be able to understand medicine labels, instructions, and warnings.

To know the difference between prescription drugs and over-the-counter drugs.

Vocabulary: Listen, Read, Say

to have a reaction to	Q-tip/swab
to fill a prescription	antidote
to make up a prescription	vitamin
to prepare a prescription	aspirin/nonaspirin (Tylenol)
to wait for a prescription	ointment/salve/cream/lotion
to need a prescription	cough medicine
to be allergic to	rash
druggist/pharmacist	cough
prescription drugs	headache
nonprescription drugs	sore throat
brand name	sore throat medicine/lozenges
generic	indigestion/heartburn/upset stomach
content(s)	insomnia
drug/medicine/medication	chapped lips
dose/dosage	sunburn
overdose (OD)	cut/sore
containers: jar, box, tube, can, bottle	pimple/blemish/acne
pill form/liquid form/tablet form	hay fever/sinus congestion/runny nose

application/applicator	nose spray
cotton/cotton ball	allergy
	poison/toxin/toxic
	antidote/ipecac syrup
	over-the-counter drugs

Structures and Skill Building

I'd like to have this prescription filled.

Could you fill this prescription for me?

I need to have this prescription filled.

What do you suggest for (ailment)?

Can you give me something for (ailment)?

Do you have any allergies?

Are you allergic to any drugs?

I think you'd better ask and/or see a doctor.

13

Health V

The Dentist

Competency Goals

To be able to give information about yourself and seek information from others with regard to dental and orthodontic services.

To be able to understand dental terminology when making a dental appointment.

Vocabulary: Listen, Read, Say

to brush/clean	filling	orthodontist
to floss	dentist	braces
to examine	oral surgeon	retainer
to treat	dental hygienist	spacers
to whiten	dental assistant	to straighten
to remove	dentist's office	root canal
to pull/extract	waiting room	preventive dentistry
to drill	mouth	dental hygiene
to rot/decay	tongue	regular checkups
to lose	gums	fluoride treatment
to fall out	wisdom tooth/teeth	injection/shot
to hurt	bridge	filling
to fill a tooth	toothache	Novocain
to get a checkup	dentures/false teeth	gas/nitrous oxide
to go to the dentist	cavity/cavities	sodium pentothal
to need an appointment	filling	painful
toothpaste	crown/cap	dental floss/tape
toothbrush	x-ray	
mouthwash	abscess	
to rinse your mouth		

Structures and Skill Building

My tooth hurts.	You need to go to the dentist.
I have a toothache.	You need to make an appointment with the dentist.
Hello. I need an appointment with Dr. _____.	What seems to be the problem?
My tooth hurts/I have a toothache.	Can you come in (day) at (time)?
Please repeat the time.	(Day) at (time).
Thank you.	You're welcome.

14

Health VI

Personal Hygiene

Competency Goals

To be able to give information about yourself and seek information from others with regard to personal hygiene.

To understand the importance of personal hygiene.

Vocabulary: Listen, Read, Say

to wash/rinse	toothbrush	mouthwash
to bathe	toothpaste	dental floss
to shower	scissors	nail clippers
to bush/comb your hair	comb	toenail clippers
to clean	brush	nail file
to sterilize	cotton/cotton ball	razor
to get a haircut	Q-tip/swab	razor blades
to check for head lice	tweezers	electric razor
	nail file	aftershave/cologne
body lotion/hand lotion		perfume
deodorant	pharmacy/drugstore	
soap	online (Amazon, etc.)	bathroom/restroom
shampoo/conditioner	supermarket	
astringent	laundromat	barber
towel/washcloth		beautician/hairdresser
clean	washer	
dirty	dryer	germs/disease
	hairdryer	
makeup	flat iron	
acne medicine/medication	hot rollers	

Structures and Skill Building

Wash your hands before cooking/eating.

Wash your hands after using/going to the bathroom/restroom.

I'd like to wash my hands.

There's a bathroom/restroom over there.

Where's the bathroom/restroom?

May I use the bathroom/restroom?

The restroom is (directions).

I need a haircut.

Will you cut my hair, please?

My clothes are dirty.

My (items of clothes) are dirty.

I need to wash my clothes.

I need to wash my (item or items).

I'll go to the Laundromat.

I'll use the washer and dryer.

Will you wash my (item/items) for me, please?

Do you take a shower/bath every day?

Yes, I take a _____ every day.

How often do you wash your hair?

I wash my hair (# of times) a week.

Do you ever check your hair for head lice?

Yes, I do check for head lice.

No, I don't check for head lice.

Don't forget to put on/use deodorant.

Be sure to brush your teeth at least twice a day and use mouthwash.

Be sure to floss your teeth every day.

File/Clip your fingernails and toenails.

Don't wear too much makeup.

Where can I buy (hygienic item)?

You can buy (hygienic item) at/a/the pharmacy (drugstore, discount store, supermarket).

15

Health VII

Emergency Services

Competency Goals

To be able to give information about yourself and seek the same from others with regard to emergency services.

To be able to communicate on the phone and in person with emergency personnel.

Emergency Services (911)

Fire

Police

Suicide Prevention

Sheriff

Ambulance

Highway Patrol

Parental Stress Life-Line

Poison Control Center

Alcohol and Drug Abuse

Abused Women's, Men's, and Children's Services

Rape Crisis Center

Vocabulary: Listen, Read, Say

Fire Department Terminology

to catch (on) fire	fire
to burn (up, down)	firefighter
to be on fire	fire department
to start a fire	firehouse
to put out a fire	fire engine/fire truck
to rescue	fire alarm box
to destroy	alarm/smoke alarm
to notify	arson/arsonist
to protect	hydrant
to asphyxiate	smoke
to escape	flame
to jump	hose/hoses

to prevent	ladder/ladders
Help!	emergency exit/fire escape
brave	siren
smoke inhalation	fireproof/flame retardant
net (for jumping into)	dangerous
burn/burns	

Police Department Terminology

police department	ticket (parking, speeding, etc.)
police station	policeman/policewoman
badge/badge number	police car/patrol car
police report	driver's license/identification/ID
victim(s)	describe/description
suspect(s)	crime/felony/misdemeanor

Ambulance and Paramedic Terminology

ambulance driver	first aid/oxygen
stretcher	medical information
CPR (cardio pulmonary resuscitation)	IV (intravenous medication)

Call Police and/or Fire Department for These Situations: 911

poisoning	drowning
heart attack	drug overdose
domestic violence/rape/abuse	theft/robbery
bodily injuries (shooting, stabbing, etc.)	other emergencies

Structures and Skill Building

There is a fire at (address).

There's an emergency at _____.

Please send an ambulance/a paramedic to (address).

We need the police at (address).

Please call the/a/an _____.

16

Money and Banking

Competency Goals

To be able to give information about yourself and seek information from others with regard to money and banking.

To be able to comprehend the American Monetary System.

To be able to make change.

To have a general knowledge of the credit card system.

To have a basic understanding of the savings and checking account systems.

To be able to comprehend the money and banking vocabulary.

Vocabulary: Listen, Read, Say

Money Terminology

currency	nickel
cash	penny
bills—small and large	
coins/coin rolls	currency
dollar	one/ones
dollar bill	five/fives
silver dollar	ten/tens
half dollar/fifty-cent piece	twenty/twenties
quarter	fifty/fifties
dime	hundred/hundreds

Banking Terminology

bank	traveler's checks
banking hours	bank card

banker	credit/debit card (line of credit)
savings and loan	vault/safe
account number(s)	safe deposit box
savings account	checkbook
checking account	interest
joint account	loan—personal/business
individual account	balance
online banking/electronic banking	to form a line
transaction(s)	to wait in line
deposit	to deposit
deposit slip	to withdraw
withdrawal	to open an account
withdrawal slip	to close an account
counter	to stop payment on a check
teller	to cash a check
teller's window	to earn interest
ATM (automated teller machine)	to borrow
ATM card (password/code)	to get/need change
receipt	to fill out
manager	to transfer from checking to savings
officer	to transfer from savings to checking
branch/office	
check/personal check	ATM identity protector case/cover
money order	
bank guard	

Identification Terminology

driver's license/driver's permit/identification card
major credit card
identity theft/stolen credit or debit card/stolen bank card

Structures and Skill Building

I'd like to open a checking/savings account.

How much would you like to deposit?

I'd like to borrow (amount).

Please fill out these forms.

What is the monthly interest on a (amount) loan?

The interest is (amount).

I'd like to withdraw (amount).

Would you like that in small or large bills?

I'd like to close my account.

Could you tell me my balance?

I'd like to cash a check.

I'd like to transfer (amount) (from my checking to my savings) (from my savings to my checking).

My bank (credit/debit card) has been stolen. What should I do?

I'm a victim of identity theft. What do I need to do?

17

Shopping I
General

Competency Goals

To be able to give information about yourself and seek information from others with regard to general shopping terminology.

To have a general understanding of the different types of sales and advertisements.

To be able to comprehend the words *layaway*, *returns*, and *credit* and to have an understanding of various exchange policies.

To be able to order from a catalog, online, and through the mail.

Vocabulary: Listen, Read, Say

to be helped	cash register	counter
to be waited on	cashier	display case
to be taken care of	salesperson	shopping cart
to look for	sales clerk / clerk	escalator
to order	manager	elevator
to order from a catalog	customer / shopper	store policy
to order online	price / price tag	layaway
to send / mail	merchandise price scanner	deposit / money down
to buy	regular price	balance
to cost	sale price	change
to spend	cost	
to charge with a credit card	on sale	bargain
to pay cash	reduced	cheap / inexpensive / expensive
to exchange / even exchange	marked down	aisle
to return / refund	online sale price	store coupons
to credit my account	in-store sale price	mail coupons

to pay	semi-annual sale	online coupons
to write a check	warehouse sale	catalogue receipt
	going-out-of-business sale	return policy
merchandise	clearance sale	no return policy
returns counter/desk	white sale	reason for return
customer service	close-out sale	
	size tag	shopping bag
	sales receipt	credit card identity protector cover/case

Structures and Skill Building

Are you being helped?

No. Could you tell me where I can find (item/items)?

Yes, please. I'm looking for _____.

May I help you?

Yes, please. Do you have a/any _____?

Is anybody/anyone helping you?

No, could you? I need a/an _____.

Do you need some help/assistance?

Yes. Could you show me (item/items)?

Yes. Could you tell me where to find (item/items)?

Is anyone/anybody taking care of you?

No, thank you. I'm just looking.

How much is/are (item/items)?

What's the price of (item/items)?

It costs (amount).

They cost (amount).

That's too much/too expensive.

I can't spend that much.

It's on sale for (amount).

They're reduced/marked down.

It's/They're free. You don't have to pay for it/them.

That's a bargain.

That's cheap/inexpensive.

How would you like to pay for this/these?

Will that be cash or charge?

I'll pay cash.

I'll write a check.

I'll charge it/them.

I'd like to exchange (item/items) for (item/items).

I'd like to return (item/items). It/They (give explanation for return).

How much did you spend/pay for that/those (item/items)?

I paid/spent (amount).

How much did that/those (item/items) cost?

It/They cost (amount).

18

Shopping II

Clothing

Competency Goals

To be able to give information about yourself and seek information from others with regard to clothing and related terminology.

To be able to identify specific clothing.

To be able to distinguish between casual and dress clothing and when to wear it.

To know the difference between a department store, specialty store, and discount store.

Vocabulary: Listen, Read, Say

Men's and Boys' Clothing

robe/bathrobe	slacks/trousers/pants
pajamas/PJs	suit/three-piece suit
underwear	vest
undershirt/t-shirt	shirt: dress/sport/rugby/polo
undershorts/jockey shorts/boxer shorts	sweater: cardigan/pullover/crewneck/turtle neck/V-neck
socks	jeans/Levi's
jacket/windbreaker	warm up suit
jacket/sport coat	sweatshirt/sweatpants/sweats
coat/overcoat	shorts/Bermuda/running
trench coat/raincoat	bathing suit/swim trunks

Ladies and Girls' Clothing

robe/bathrobe	formal/semiformal
pajamas/PJs	suit
nightgown	jacket/blazer

lingerie	jumpsuit/pantsuit
slip/half-slip	slacks/pants
bra	leggings/jeggings
underpants/underwear	jeans/Levi's
teddy	skirt: long, mid-calf (midi)/mini
blouse/shirt	trench coat/raincoat
t-shirt	nylons/pantyhose/knee-high stockings
tank top/tank	socks/knee socks/tights
warm-up suit/sweat suit/sweats	shorts/Bermuda/running
sweater/cardigan/turtleneck	swimsuit: two-piece/one-piece (tank)/bikini/ tankini
dress/jumper	
cocktail dress	

Fabrics

cotton	denim
wool	linen
polyester	knit
rayon	blends
nylon	leather

Related Terminology

color/colors	dry clean only
size/sizes: petite, small, medium, large, extra-large, 2X, 3X, etc.	hand wash only
one size fits all	to care for
one size fits most	to tight, loose, small, big, wide, narrow
aisle	garment
rack	pair of _____
dressing/fitting room(s)	to try on/put on
alteration/alterations	to fit/not fit
dressmaker/seamstress/tailor	to want
long-sleeved/short-sleeved	to prefer
label/tag	to match

brand name/manufacturer's name/generic	to take off
price tag/size tag	to wear
machine washable	to take out/to take in (alterations)

Stores

department stores	shoe stores
specialty shops	discount stores
boutiques	sporting goods stores

Structures and Skill Building

May I help you?

Yes, please. I'd like to try on this/these (item/items).

What size do you wear?

I wear size _____.

The size(s) you want is/are on this/that rack.

Thank you.

What color do you prefer?

I'd like the navy blue one/ones.

Where's the fitting/dressing room?

It's (give directions).

It fits, but the (item/items) need to be shortened.

It fits, but the (item/items) are too long.

We have free alterations. Just one minute and I'll call the seamstress/tailor.

Thank you.

Will this/that be cash or charge?

Charge.

Thank you. I hope you enjoy your new (item/items).

19

Shopping III

Accessories

Competency Goals

To be able to give information about yourself and seek information from others with regard to accessories.

To be able to identify specific accessories.

Vocabulary: Listen, Read, Say

Men's and Boys' Accessories

shoes	handkerchief
tennis shoes/running shoes/cross trainers	umbrella
sandals/flip flops	briefcase
loafers/moccasins	wallet/billfold
boots	jewelry
dress shoes	chain
slippers	bracelet/ID bracelet
belt/belt buckle	ring
tie/bow tie	buttons
tie clip/tie tack	headband/wristband(s)
cuff links	
hat/cap	precious stone(s)
scarf	gold/silver/platinum (referring to jewelry)
gloves/mittens	
watch	
glasses/sunglasses	earring/earrings (pierced) (post/hoop)

Ladies' and Girls' Accessories

shoes	hat/cap
heels (high/medium/low)	glasses/sunglasses
flats	jewelry
boots	earrings (stud/hoop/dangle) (pierced/clip)
slippers	necklace
sandals/flip flops	bracelet/bangle
loafers/moccasins	chain
tennis shoes/running shoes/cross trainers	pendant
purse/bag/handbag	pin
shoulder bag	ring
cross-body bag	ankle bracelet
clutch purse	toe ring
gloves/mittens	buttons
wallet/coin purse	umbrella
handkerchief	briefcase
scarf	headband/wristband(s)
belt/belt buckle	hairclips/ribbons/bows

Structures and Skill Building

May I show you a wallet?

Yes, please. I'd like to see those two black leather ones in the case.

Of course. Here you are. Aren't they beautiful? They're 100 percent leather.

This one is (amount). And this one is (amount).

They're very expensive.

Yes, but leather is very expensive.

I think I'll look around. Thank you for your help.

20

Shopping IV

The Supermarket

Competency Goals

To be able to give information about yourself and seek information from others with regard to general grocery shopping in the supermarket and in small grocery stores.

To have a knowledge of and an understanding of the aisles and sections in a supermarket.

To understand the use of coupons and how to comparison shop.

To be able to make a grocery list.

To be able to ask directions on how to fink an item.

To be able to read and understand supermarket advertisements/ads.

Vocabulary: Listen, Read, Say

to make a list	cash register	shopping cart
to go grocery shopping	cashier/checker	pushcart/cart
to shop	clerk	basket
to park	bagger	scale(s)
to buy	checkout counter	
to add up the bill	checkout stand	fresh
to pay the bill	line	frozen
to get in line	list/grocery list	fresh-frozen
to weigh	shelf/shelves	
to choose	carton	receipt
to pick out	can	paper bag/plastic bag
to compare prices	package	coupon(s)
to check out	bottle	
to self-checkout	jar	aisle

to look at/read ads	box	
to cut out coupons	bag/sack	Excuse me.
to print out coupons	loaf/slice	How much is/are _____?
to need	bar	Where's/Where are _____?
to pick up a few things	head	Where can I find _____?
to check off your list	bunch	Can you tell me where I can find _____?
to write a check	gallon	
to pay cash	half-gallon	
to pay with a credit card/to swipe your credit card	quart	
to need help	pint(s)	
to buy in balk	ounce(s)	
	pound(s)	
	dozen/half dozen	
	organic	

Common Sections/Departments

wine/liquor/beer	ethnic foods/Hispanic/Asian
juices/soft drinks	baking mix/preserves
dairy: milk/butter/margarine/yogurt/cheese/eggs	baby needs/diapers/formula/food
light bulb/household	spices/coffee/tea
cleansers/detergents	frozen foods
pet food/pet supplies	ice cream/frozen desserts
paper products/paper towels/toilet paper	frozen breakfasts/dinners
bread/grains/cereals	pasta: macaroni/spaghetti
canned vegetables/fruit	condiments: mayonnaise/mustard/ketchup
meat department/delicatessen (deli)	seafood department
soup/cookies/crackers	frozen pizza/frozen ethnic foods
frozen vegetables/fruit	produce department
frozen dinners/diet food	bakery department
candy/drugs/feminine hygiene	generic section

Structures and Skill Building

Before Shopping

I need to pick up a few things at the supermarket/grocery store.

What do you need?

I need milk, eggs, bread, margarine, and coffee.

You'd better make a list so you don't forget anything.

I will.

At the Supermarket

Excuse me. Where's the bread?

Where can I find the bread?

Can you tell me where I can find the bread?

It's in Aisle 3a.

It's in Aisle 3a next to the _____.

Thanks.

At the Meat Department

How much is the ground beef today?

It's $0.99 per pound.

I'd like a pound, please.

Will that be all?

Yes.

That will be $0.99. Please pay the cashier/checker.

Thank you.

At the Checkout

Here are my coupons.

Your total is/comes to $37.50.

Minus your coupons, that makes it $35.90.

Here you are (cash/check/swipe credit card).

Structures and Skill Building

May I see your driver's license/ID/identification, please?

Thank you. Do you need some help out to your car?

No, thank you.

Yes, please. My car is parked far away.

21

Shopping V

Specific Foods

Competency Goals

To be able to give information about yourself and seek information from others with regard to specific foods.

To be able to identify specific foods and food groups.

To be able to make a grocery list of specific foods.

To know how to use coupons and how to comparison shop.

To know the four major food groups: *milk, meat, vegetables and fruits*, and *breads and cereals*.

Vocabulary: Listen, Read, Say

Dairy Products

milk (varieties)	yogurt
cream	cream cheese
	sour cream
half and half	cheese (varieties)
eggs	cottage cheese
butter	ice cream
margarine	ice milk
whipping cream	

Meat/Fish/Poultry

hamburger (ground beef)	chicken (parts)
ham	turkey (parts)
pork (varieties)	duck (parts)
beef (varieties)	
lamb (varieties)	fish (varieties)
veal (varieties)	shellfish

ribs (pork or beef)	shrimp
sausages (varieties)	crab
bacon	lobster
liver	clams
	mussels
various cuts of meat	oysters

Fruits

apples	papaya
oranges	rhubarb
grapefruit	grapes (varieties)
nectarines	cherries (varieties)
tangerines	berries (varieties)
peaches	mangos
pears	kiwi
plums	bananas
apricots	pineapple
melons (varieties)	limes
lemons	avocado

Vegetables

lettuce (varieties)	zucchini
cabbage	mushrooms
spinach	radishes
tomatoes	beets
carrots	turnips
celery	corn
cucumbers	artichokes
onions (varieties)	beans (varieties)
potatoes (varieties)	peas
peas	peppers
peppers	broccoli
broccoli	asparagus
asparagus	squash (varieties)

Breads/Rice/Pasta/Cereal

bread (varieties)	cakes
rolls/buns	pies
donuts/doughnuts (varieties)	dry cereal (varieties)
pastries (varieties)	oatmeal
crackers (varieties)	Cream of Wheat
rice (varieties)	Cream of Rice
pasta (varieties)	hot/cold cereal
cookies	cooked/uncooked cereal

Related Terminology

measurements and weights of items	diet
low calorie	balanced diet
high calorie	calorie counting
nutrition/nutritional	four food groups
commercially grown	organically grown

Structures and Skill Building

What's your favorite (category of food)?

My favorite _____ is _____.

What are your favorite (category of food)?

My favorite _____ are _____.

What/Which (category of food, singular/plural) do you dislike?

I dislike/don't like (category of food, singular/plural).

Make a shopping list for one day.

What items are in your list?

How many fruits and vegetables can you name?

What foods are *low calorie*?

What foods are *high calorie*?

What does the word *calorie* mean?

How much is/are (item) at (store)?

22

Meals

Competency Goals

To be able to give information about yourself and seek information from others with regard to preparing, setting up, and creating various meals.

To know what a balanced diet is.

To be able to make up three nutritional (balanced) meals: breakfast, lunch, and dinner.

To be able to read and understand a recipe.

Vocabulary: Listen, Read, Say

Breakfast

eggs (varieties)	jam/jelly
juice (varieties)	breakfast sandwich
milk	toast (varieties)
coffee	muffins (varieties)
tea	yogurt
hot chocolate/cocoa	grits
hot or cold cereal (varieties)	bagels
waffles	ham
pancakes	sausage (link/patty)
French toast	bacon
syrup	hash browns
butter	country potatoes
margarine	instant breakfast drinks

Lunch

sandwich (varieties)	fruit (varieties)
soup	tacos

chips (varieties)	dessert: cake, pie, cookies
French fries	ice cream (varieties)
onion rings	ice cream bar (varieties)
hot dog	popsicles/juice bars/yogurt bars
hamburger/cheeseburger	frozen yogurt
chili burger/chili dog	beverages (varieties)
salad	
salad dressing (varieties)	
pizza	

Condiments

ketchup	hot sauce
mustard	steak sauce
mayonnaise	pickles
relish	

Dinner

meat/fish/poultry	pasta (varieties)
potatoes (varieties)	bread/rolls
vegetables (varieties)	butter/margarine
salad/salad dressing(s)	beverage (varieties)
rice (varieties)	dessert (varieties)

Related Terminology

to set the table	tablecloth
napkins	placemats
dishes/plates	salt and pepper (shakers)
salad plates	
bowels	to prepare
soup bowls	to cook
cup	to make breakfast, lunch, dinner
saucer	to clear
glass	to do the dishes
bread and butter plate	to diet/to be on a diet
silverware	to gain weight/to lose weight

fork	balanced diet / unbalanced diet
knife	nutritious meal
spoon	cookbook / recipe(s)
teaspoon	dishwasher
tablespoon	to load / put the dishes in the dishwasher
soupspoon	to unload / take out the dishes
chopsticks	

Structures and Skill Building

What did you have for breakfast this morning?

I had _____.

What did you have for lunch yesterday?

I had _____.

What's in your lunch today?

There's / There are _____.

What did you have for dinner last night?

I had _____.

What would you like to have for dinner tonight?

I'd like to have _____.

Who makes / prepares breakfast at your house?

_____ prepares breakfast at my house.

Who sets the table for dinner?

_____ sets the table for dinner.

Who clears the table / dishes?

_____ does / washes the dishes.

Does someone wash the dishes or load / put them in the dishwasher?

_____ loads / puts them in the dishwasher.

_____ does them.

What should you eat for (breakfast, lunch, dinner) if you're on a diet?

If I'm on a diet, I shouldn't eat _____ for (meal).

What should you eat for (breakfast, lunch, dinner) if you want to gain weight?

If I want to gain weight, I should eat _____ for (meal).

What is a *balanced diet/meal*?

What is nutritious food?

23

At the Restaurant

Competency Goals

To be able to give information about yourself and seek information from others with regard to a meal in a restaurant.

To be able to make a reservation.

To be able to read and order from a menu.

To be able to read and understand the check/bill.

To be able to order at a fast-food restaurant in person and at the drive-thru.

Vocabulary: Listen, Read, Say

to make a reservation	cloakroom/checkroom
to have a reservation	chef/cook
to be seated	cocktail/drink
to follow	appetizer/hors d'oeuvre
to put your napkin on your lap	soup and/or salad
to order	main course/entree
to leave a tip	dessert
to pay the cashier/waiter/waitress/server	beverage
How many in your party?	dinner or a la carte
Walk this way.	side order
Right this way.	wine list
Follow me.	menu
host/hostess/maître d'	specialties of the house/house specials
waiter/waitress/server	meal
cocktail waitress/waiter/server	bill/check/bar tab
busboy	tax

cashier	tip
counter	restroom(s)/bathroom(s)
table/chairs	ladies' room/men's room
booth	
bar stools/stools	How would you like your meat cooked?
place setting	rare, medium, well done
salt and pepper	
cream and sugar	spicy/hot/mild
sugar substitute	
glass of water	fast-food restaurant (McDonald's, Taco Bell, etc.)
silverware: knife, fork, spoon	Here or to go?
napkin	here—tray
tablecloth	to go/to take out—bag
placemat	drive-thru restaurant
	ethnic restaurant

Structures and Skill Building

Making a Reservation

May I help you?

Yes. I'd like to make a reservation for this/next Friday for dinner.

How many (in your party)?

Four.

And what time?

7:30.

And your name, please?

O'Sullivan, Johnny.

Thank you, Mr. O' Sullivan. We'll see you at 7:30 on Friday, (date).

Thank you. Good-bye.

Arriving at the Restaurant

Hello. May I help you? (Do you have a reservation?)

Yes, I have a reservation for four at 7:30.

And the (your) name, please?

O'Sullivan. Johnny O'Sullivan

Yes, Mr. O'Sullivan. We have your reservation. The host/hostess will seat you.

Yes, Mr. O'Sullivan. We have your reservation. Right this way, please. (Follow me, please.)

Thank you.

Ordering

Would you like/care for a cocktail/drink before (name of meal)?

No, thank you. We'd like to see the menu.

Certainly. Your waiter/waitress/server will be right with you.

Thank you.

Good afternoon/evening. (Waiter/waitress/server hands out menus.)

Besides our regular menu, we have a few specials. They are _____.

Thank you. I'd like the prime rib.

And how would you like that done/cooked?

Medium, please.

Would you like soup or salad?

Salad, please.

And what kind of dressing?

Blue cheese.

And to drink?

A glass of white wine.

Thank you.

At the End of the Meal

Will there be anything else? Will that be all?

Yes, thank you. We'd like the check, please.

Certainly. Here you are. Please pay the cashier. (*Note*: If the check is brought to you on a tray, put the money on the tray and the waiter/waitress/server will pick it up, give it to the cashier for payment, and he/she will return your change to you.)

Thank you.

Fast-Food Restaurant

May I help you?/Next please.

I'd like a cheeseburger, a large order of fries, and a chocolate shake.

A large or small shake?

Small.

Will that be "for here" or "to go"?/"Here" or "to go"?

To go, please.

That's/That will be $7.25.

(Give a ten-dollar bill.)

Out of ten dollars/Out of ten. $2.75 is your change. Thank you.

24

Sports and Sports Equipment

Competency Goals

To be able to give information about yourself and seek information from others with regard to sports, sports equipment, and sportsmanship.

To be able to identify specific sports.

To be able to identify sports equipment and the sport for which it is used.

To be able to comprehend sports terminology.

To know the difference between the amateur athlete and the professional athlete (amateur status and professional status).

Vocabulary: Listen Read, Say

Team and Individual Sports

football	body surfing	horse racing
baseball	jet skiing	bowling
basketball	swimming	golf
soccer	synchronized swimming	handball
rugby	diving	tennis
track and field	water polo	racquetball
boating	polo	skateboarding
rowing	hiking/mountain climbing	volleyball
canoeing	gymnastics	biking
sailing	hockey (ice/field)	fishing
water skiing	running/jogging	aerobic dance
snow skiing	boxing	aerobics
snowboarding	fencing	judo
crew	wrestling	karate

weight training	skating (ice/roller)	weightlifting
lacrosse	skimboarding	rhythmic gymnastics
biking	scuba diving	extreme sports
surfing	skin diving	ultimate fighting
wind surfing	horseback riding/equestrian	trampoline
ping pong	archery	

Sports Equipment

facemask	floor mats
helmet	bowling pins
knee pads	bowling ball
shoulder pads	weights
shin guards	weight machines
cleats	treadmill
racket/racquet/paddle	elliptical
hat/cap	stationary bike
paddle/oar	bindings (snow skiing/snowboarding)
water skis	uniform
snow skis	jersey
snowboard	t-shirt
poles (snow skiing)	ball (varieties)
surfboard	mitt/glove (varieties)
body board	mouthpiece/mouthguard
uneven bars	net/backboard/rim
balance beam	hoop/basket
horse/vaulting	goalpost/uprights
bat/stick	net
puck	saber/foil
hurdles (low and high)	boxing gloves
discus	javelin
shot put	universal gym
pads (varieties—other than knee and shoulder)	club (golf)
saddle	bow and arrow/bullseye/target

Related Terminology

to participate	game/contest/match/meet	goalie
to play	event/sport/tournament	catcher
to win	athlete	end zone
to lose	opponent/rival/rivalry	base
to tie	athletic/team/club	baseline
to score	fan/spectator	error(s)
to throw	player/participant	pitcher's mound
to catch	referee/umpire	batter's box
to pass	rule/rules	dugout
to shoot	point(s)/goal(s)/run(s)/score	team bench
to swing	tie/draw	"on deck"
to watch/to spectate	dead heat	on deck circle
to be a "good sport"	forfeit/default	bullpen
to be a "bad sport"	overtime/double overtime	Pan American Games
to race	sudden death	Olympic Games
to intercept	finish line	Super Bowl
to kick	goal line	World Series
to run	yard line	World Cup
to bat	amateur status	The Master's
to hit	professional status	The U.S. Open (golf/tennis)
to pitch	famous/popular	Wimbledon
to walk	dangerous	The Pro Bowl
to balk	exciting	The All-Star Game
to tag/to tag out	sportsmanship	Playoffs/championships
to set	unsportsmanlike conduct	Quarter finals/semifinals
to spike	football season	Bowl Championship Series
to jog	baseball season	
to serve	basketball season	
to block	snow season	
to sack	rink	
to punch	ring	
to tackle	stadium/coliseum	
to pin	field	

to foul	strike	
to foul back	spare	
to strike out	split	
to exercise/to get exercise	gymnasium/gym	
to train	bleachers	
to work out	stands	
to row/to paddle	"live"	
to save	prerecorded	
to go/step out of bounds	goalpost	

Structures and Skill Building

What sports are you good at?

I'm good at _____.

What's your favorite *participant* sport?

My favorite *participant* sport is _____.

What position do you usually play?

I usually play _____?

What's your favorite position?

My favorite position is _____.

What is your favorite *spectator* sport?

My favorite *spectator* sport is _____.

Do you like to watch (sport)?

Yes, I like to watch _____.

No, I don't like to watch _____.

Have you ever gone to a live (sport) game/match/contest?

Yes, I have gone to a live _____.

No, I haven't gone to a live _____.

Where was it?

It was at/in (place).

What equipment is used in (sport)?

(Equipment) is/are used in _____.

How do you feel when you win a _____?

I feel _____ when I win a _____.

How do you feel when you lose a _____?

I feel _____ when I lose a _____.

Are you a *good sport* when you participate?

What is a *good sport*?

Who is your favorite athlete?

_____ is my favorite athlete.

Is he/she a *good sport*? Why?

Yes, he/she is a good sport because _____.

No, he/she isn't a good sport because _____.

Who is your favorite *amateur* athlete?

Who is your favorite *professional* athlete?

25

Feelings and Emotions

Competency Goals

To be able to give information about yourself and seek information from others with regard to your feelings and emotions.

To be able to identify emotions and/or expressions.

To be able to write about how you feel.

To be able to understand emotion(s).

Vocabulary: Listen, Read, Say

To Feel

sad	sadness
happy	happiness
angry	anger
frustrated	frustration
depressed	depression
anxious	anxiety
nervous	nervousness
worried	worry
mad	madness
upset	
intelligent	intelligent
smart	
dumb	
stupid	stupidity

73

adequate	adequacy
confident	confidence (able)
not confident	no confidence (unable)
certain	uncertain
sure	unsure
inadequate	inadequacy
defeat	defeated
undefeated	
content	contentment
discontent	discontentment
proud	pride
victorious	victory
alone/lonely	loneliness
rejected	rejection
accepted	acceptance
confused	confusion
disoriented	disorientation
puzzled	
embarrassed	embarrassment
bored	boredom
disappointed	disappointment
hurt	
frightened	fright
scared	fear
afraid	unafraid
in love	love
romantic	romance

jealous	jealousy
annoyed	annoyance
bothered	bother
irritated	irritation
guilty	guilt
tired	
sleepy	
hungry	hunger
thirsty	thirst

Structures and Skill Building

How do you feel after you pass a test?

I feel (emotion).

How do you feel after flunking a test?

I feel (emotion).

How do you feel during a test when you haven't studied the material?

I feel (emotion).

How do you feel after winning a game/match/contest?

I feel (emotion).

How do you feel after losing a game/match/contest?

I feel (emotion).

How do you feel when someone close to you gets sick?

I feel (emotion).

Do you think it's OK to cry sometimes? Why? When?

Yes, I think it's OK to cry sometimes. (Explanation).

No, I don't think it's OK to cry. (Explanation).

How do you feel when you can't do something?

I feel (emotion).

How do you *handle/deal* with the situation?

I (explanation).

26

Leisure Time I

Hobbies, Activities, and Interests at Home

Competency Goals

To be able to give information about yourself and seek information from others with regard to leisure time activities in the home.

To be able to write a letter by hand or on the computer.

To understand the values of television and computer devices and their limitations.

To become familiar with American hobbies, activities, and interests in the home.

Vocabulary: Listen, Read, Say

General Terminology

to watch television/TV	to draw/paint/sculpt
to rent a movie/DVD/Blu-ray	to play ball/to play catch
to listen to the radio	to sew/crochet/knit
to listen to an iPod/mp3 player	to play a game/sport/musical instrument
to read	
to garden	to ride your bike/scooter/skateboard
to play computer games	to shoot hoops
to play cards	to play "strike out"
to write a letter	
to collect stamps	download games/movies
to build models	camera
to wash the car	board games (Monopoly/chess/checkers)
to wash the dog	to do a puzzle (crossword or jigsaw)
to plan a party	photography/download or upload photos
to plan a picnic	

to plan a vacation	free time
to take a nap	leisure time

To Watch TV

television /flat screen/high definition (hi-def)	series	sports (news/events/games)
program	game show	commercials
channel	soap opera/soaps	broadcast
remote	mystery	documentary
volume	western	special
to change the channel	comedy	drama
cable/dish	sci-fi (science fiction)	realty TV
to record a program	talk show	educational programming (PBS)
to set a reminder	news	movie ratings: G/PG/PG-13/R/NC-17
to save a recording	music	TV/program blocking

The Computer/Computer Devices

computer (desktop/laptop/tablet)	printer/scanner/copier
iPod/MP3 player	applications
computer games	browser (Google, Yahoo)
computer hardware/software	bug /virus
keyboard	to download/upload
mouse	to hack/to be hacked
modem	identity theft
Internet provider	online/offline
Internet	compose letter
email	contacts
chat rooms	compose letter/cc/bcc
website/webpage	attachments/files/folders
social media/social networking (Twitter, Facebook, etc.)	Bluetooth sync (synchronize)
password/sign in	

To Write a Letter

stationary / paper	address / return address
envelope	stamp / postage

To Play Cards

deck of cards	face cards (king / queen / jack)
suits (hearts / diamonds / spades / clubs)	dealer
card games: poker, rummy, gin rummy, hearts, go fish, casino, canasta, bridge, black jack, etc.	score / to keep score
points	to bet / to place a / your bet
score pad	to make a bet
chips	

Structures and Skill Building

What do you like to do with / in your leisure / free time at home?

I like to _____ with / in my leisure / free time at home.

Do you have a hobby or special interest you do at home?

Yes, I do. I (explain).

No, I don't have a hobby / special interest.

How much TV do you watch on a school day?

I watch (amount) hours of TV on a school day?

How much TV do you watch on a weekend?

I watch (amount) hours of TV on the weekend.

What are your favorite programs?

My favorite programs are _____.

Do you think you learn anything from watching TV? What?

Yes, I think I learn (explanation) from watching TV.

No, I don't think I learn anything from watching TV.

Does watching TV help your English?

Yes, watching TV helps my English.

No, watching TV doesn't help my English.

How much time do you spend on your computer?

I spend (hours) on my computer.

What do you like to do most on your computer?

I like to do (explain) on my computer.

Do you watch movies and/or play games on your computer?

Yes, I watch movies and/or play games on my computer.

No, I don't watch movies and/or play games on my computer.

Which movies do you watch? Which games do you play?

I watch (explain). I play (explain).

Does your mother/father/sister/brother have a hobby or special interest at home?

Yes, my mother/father/sister/brother (explain) at home.

No, my mother/father/sister/brother doesn't have a hobby or special interest at home.

What hobby would you like to try if you could?

I'd like to try (explain).

Do you play a musical instrument?

Yes, I do. I play the (name of instrument).

No, I don't.

Would you like to play a musical instrument? Which one?

Yes, I'd like to play the (name of instrument).

No, I wouldn't.

Do you play any card or board games? Which ones?

Yes, I play (name of card/board game(s)).

No, I don't.

27

Leisure Time II

Hobbies, Activities, and Interests Away from Home

Competency Goals

To be able to give information about yourself and seek information from others with regard to leisure time activities outside the home.

To become familiar with American hobbies, activities, and interests away from home.

Vocabulary: Listen, Read, Say

General Terminology

to go to the movies	camp
museum/aquarium	biking/bike ride
symphony	jet ski
opera	scuba/skin dive
theater	surf/body surf
library	
park	to go shopping
beach	to go on a picnic
river	to pack a lunch
sporting events: football/baseball/basketball	
	to attend/go to a concert
carnival/fair/circus	to go to a party
	to go to a dance
to horseback ride	to go "out"
fish	to go "out for the evening"
hunt	
boat	
water ski	
swim	

To Fish/To Go Fishing

fisherman	knapsack/backpack
fishing pole/rod	boots
reel	tackle box
line	boat
hook/fly	pier
bait	off shore
net	lake/ocean

To Go to a Concert

pop/rock group	speakers
singer(s)	drums/cymbals
lead singer	tambourine
background singers	piano/organ
microphone	concert hall
guitar	amphitheater
amplifier	stage
tickets/to buy tickets	to buy tickets online

To Go to the Movies/Show

to buy a ticket	screen
to wait in line	movie ratings: G/PG/PG-13/R/NC-17)
to go to the snack bar	usher
to buy popcorn, candy, drinks etc.	seats/aisle
to find a seat	actor(s)/actress(es)
to be quiet	restrooms
	3D
	surround sound
cinema	curtains
restrictions	no smoking

To Go to the Park

swings	benches
slides	to sit or play on the lawn and/or grass

sandbox	play stations
picnic tables	to climb stairs/ladder
grill/to barbecue	to hang/to swing

To Go to the Library

to check out a book	bookshelf/bookshelves
to return a book	table
library card	"Quiet, Please"
librarian	due date
overdue book/fine for overdue book	computer catalog/database
e-books (electronic books)	barcode

To Go to the Theater

to buy a ticket	wings
to show your ticket	curtain
to go to your seat	spotlight
to take your seat	gallery
to buy a program	balcony
stage	orchestra
actor(s)/actress(es)	orchestra pit
cast	footlight
set	conductor

To Go to the Symphony

symphony/orchestra	conductor
musician/player	rostrum
	baton
strings (string instruments):	sheet music
violin	
bass	piano
cello	keys/keyboard
harp	organ
viola	bench

bass	stool
harp	
wind instruments (horns):	percussion
trumpet	drums
trombone	symbols
saxophone	
French horn	
flute	
clarinet	
coronet	
piccolo	
tuba	

To Go to the Beach

to swim / to go swimming	river
to go for a swim	land
to float	shore
to tread water	wave
to sink	
to drown	to sunbathe
to surf	to get a suntan / to get sunburn
to bodysurf	to windsurf
salt water	to paddleboard
fresh water	to sail
lifeguard	no lifeguard on duty / lifeguard on duty
sand	Warning: Dangerous Undertow!
suntan lotion / oil	dangerous or strong current
sunblock	whirlpool
sunglasses	surf / whitewater
ocean	raft / buoy / markers
sea	first aid kit
lake	beach towel

To Go on a Picnic

to pack / to pack a lunch	paper:
to unpack	cups
to clean up	napkins
to throw away	tablecloth
to barbeque	plates
to roast	
to grill	ants
charcoal / briquettes / propane	picnic basket
	shopping bags
plastic:	blanket
cups	picnic table
forks	benches
knives	cooler
spoons	thermos
tablecloth	insect repellant
glasses	picnic food

Structures and Skill Building

What do you like to do in / with your free / leisure time away from home?

I like to (explain).

Have you ever gone to a concert? Where was it? Who did you see?

Yes, I've gone to a concert. It was in / at (place). I saw (name of person / group).

No, I haven't / I've never gone to a concert.

Have you ever gone on a picnic? Where?

Yes, I've gone on a picnic to (place).

No, I've never / I haven't ever gone on a picnic.

What kinds of food do you like to take on a picnic?

I like to take (foods).

What supplies do you usually take on a picnic?

I take (supplies).

Have you ever gone to the beach? Where?

Yes, I've gone to the beach (name of beach) at / in (place).

No, I've never/I haven't ever gone to the beach.

What do you usually take to the beach?

I take (supplies).

How often do you go to the movies?

I go to the movies (amount).

I never go to the movies.

I rarely go to the movies.

Where do you like to sit when you go to the movies?

I like to sit (location).

What's the last movie you've seen? When did you see it? Did you like it? Why?

I saw (name of movie) (when).

Yes, I liked it because (reason).

No, I didn't like it because (reason).

Have you ever gone to a *live performance* at the theater? What was it? Where?

Yes, I've gone to (name of show) at (name of theater).

No, I haven't.

Did you like it? Why?

Yes, I liked it because (reason).

No, I didn't like it because (reason).

Have you ever gone to a zoo? Where?

Yes, I've gone to the zoo (name of zoo) in (location).

No, I haven't ever gone to a zoo.

What was your favorite animal? Why?

My favorite animal was the (name) because (reason).

Have you ever gone to a library outside school? How often did/do you go?

Yes, I've gone to a library outside school. I go/went (amount of time).

No, I haven't gone to a library outside school.

Have you ever gone fishing? Where? With whom? Did you catch anything?

Yes, I've gone fishing at/in (name of body of water) with (name of person). I caught (explain).

No, I didn't catch anything.

Have you ever gone camping? Where? With whom? Did you like it? Why?

Yes, I've gone camping at/in (name of location) with (name of person). Yes, I liked it because (reason).

No, I didn't like it because (reason).

Do you go to many parties? What kind?

Yes, I go to parties (explain).

Yes, I go to (type) parties.

No, I haven't ever gone to any parties.

No, I don't go to any parties.

No, I never go to any parties.

Have you ever gone to a dance? Where? Do you like to dance?

Yes, I've gone to a dance (dances) at (place).

I like/love/don't like to dance.

28

Living Quarters/Dwellings I

Competency Goals

To be able to give information about yourself and seek information from others with regard to various types of locations of living quarters/dwellings.

To have a complete understanding of the vocabulary.

To be able to describe your home and/or neighborhood verbally and in writing.

Vocabulary: Listen, Read, Say

country	tenant/renter
state	landlord
county/parish	
city	for sale
town	for rent
suburb	for lease
military base	
mountains	rent to own
desert	option to buy
beach	
inner city	home/house
tenement housing/low-income housing/ghetto	apartment/apartment building
retirement community	duplex
	cooperative/co-op
studio	condominium/condo
flat	dormitory/dorm
loft	rooming house/boarding house
	townhouse
	hotel

an "add-on"	motel
an addition (to a room or a house)	ranch / farm
	cottage
to sell	cabin
to own	trailer / motor home / trailer park
to lease / rent	tent
to share / time share	hostel
living quarters	roommate
dwelling	neighborhood
gated community	
property assessment	

Structures and Skill Building

Where do you live?

I live in (location) in the city of (name).

What type of dwelling do you live in?

I live in a/an (type of dwelling).

Does your family own the (type of dwelling)?

They / We (own / rent) the (type of dwelling).

Who lives with you?

My _____ and _____ lives / live with me.

Do you know any of your neighbors? Who? Tell me about them.

Yes, I know _____. (describe).

No, I don't know any of my neighbors.

Do you like your neighborhood? Why or why not?

Yes, I like my neighborhood because (explain).

No, I don't like my neighborhood because (explain).

How long have you lived there?

I've / We've lived there _____.

Where did you live in your native country?

I lived in (location).

What type of dwelling did you live in?

I lived in a/an _____.

Who lived with you?

My _____ and (etc.) lived with me.

Did you know any of your neighbors? Who? Tell me about them?

Yes, I knew _____ (describe).

No, I didn't know any of my neighbors.

How long did you live there?

I/We lived there _____.

29

Living Quarters/Dwellings II

Competency Goals

To be able to give information about yourself and seek information from others with regard to general terminology about the inside and outside of your living quarters and renting versus owning.

To be able to identify various parts of the house.

To understand the difference between renting and buying.

Vocabulary: Listen, Read, Say

hall/corridor	roof	elevator
living room	chimney	entrance
dining room	ceiling	lobby
kitchen	floor	doorman
bedroom	wall	mailbox
bathroom	window	doorbell/door knocker
guest room	window frame	keyhole
den	windowpane	chain lock
study	windowsill	dead bolt
library	shutters	
family room	awning	fire escape
game room	drainpipe	fire alarm
recreation room	gutter	smoke detector
basement	door	balcony
attic	sliding glass door	
laundry room	screen door	storeroom
patio	stairs	
porch	closets	intercom

balcony		
yard	incinerator	foyer
fence	furnace	
gate	hot water heater	mansion
garage/carport	thermostat	modest
lawn/grass	fuse box	luxurious
garden	floor plan	big/small
swimming pool/spa/hot tub	floors	complex
	ground level	gated/enclosed complex
landlord	first floor (etc.)	
tenant	story	
supervisor	one story	
manager	second story (etc.)	
utilities	two story/split level	
to include		
security deposit	ranch style	
first and last month's rent	colonial	
rent/lease	modern	
mortgage	country	
loan	Mediterranean	
down payment		
monthly payments		
principal		
interest		
taxes		
insurance (various types)		

Structures and Skill Building

How many rooms are there in your (type of dwelling)?

There are _____ rooms in my _____.

What are they?

There's the/a/an _____, _____, etc.

Do you have a yard? Where?

Yes, I/we have a yard/backyard in/on (location).

Is there a patio?

Yes, there's a patio.

No, there isn't a patio.

Is there a laundry room in your building? If not, where do you do your laundry?

Yes, there is a laundry room in my/our building.

No, there isn't a laundry room in my/our building. I/We do our laundry at (location).

Do you have a garage? Is it attached or unattached to your building?

Yes, we have a garage. It is attached/unattached to our building.

No, we don't have a garage.

If you don't have a garage, where do your parents park their car?

My parents park their car (location).

My parents don't have a car.

Is your (type of dwelling) one story or two story?

My/Our (type of dwelling) is _____.

Is it an old or new (type of dwelling)?

It's an/a (old/new) dwelling.

Do you think it is better to rent or to buy a/an (type of dwelling)? Why?

I think it is better to (answer and explain).

If you buy a/an (type of dwelling) who do you pay each month?

If I buy a/an (type of dwelling), I pay the bank/savings and loan each month.

If you rent a/an (type of dwelling) who do you pay each month?

If I rent a/an (type of dwelling) I pay the owner(s)/landlord/company who owns the building.

Why is it important to get insurance whether you rent or buy a dwelling?

It is important to get insurance because (reason).

If you are moving, what must you do?

If I'm moving I have to (explain).

30

Rooms in the Home I

Living Room, Dining Room, Hall, and Corridor

Competency Goals

To be able to give information about yourself and seek information from others with regard to the hall and corridor, and the living and dining room furnishings.

To be able to draw basic floor plans of the rooms studied and label the furniture within those rooms.

To be able to identify objects in the living room, dining room, hall and corridor.

Vocabulary: Listen, Read, Say

Living Room

sofa / couch / love seat	andirons
cushions / pillows	TV / entertainment center
armchair / recliner	pictures
end table	carpet (wall to wall) / rug / area rug
coffee table / cocktail table	draperies / drapes
lamp / lighting	curtains
fireplace	shutters
mantel	shelf / shelves

Dining Room/Area

dining room table	silver
chairs	crystal / stemware
tablecloth	coffee / tea service
placemats	carpet (wall to wall) / rug / area rug
candles	draperies / drapes / curtains
candlesticks	shutters
centerpiece	chandelier / lights

china cabinet//hutch	napkins
china	napkin rings

Hall and Corridor

door	intercom
screen door	staircase
lock and chain	landing
dead bolt (lock)	bannister
hinge	upstairs
doormat	downstairs
floor: tile/hardwood/linoleum	light switch
smoke alarm/fire alarm	house security system
stairs	hallway
rug/carpet	corridor
coatrack	foyer
hall/entry	

General Terminology

to spend time (in the living/dining room)	occasion/special occasion
piece of furniture	separate dining room
to have company/guests	to connect
"good" china/silver/crystal	to pass through

Structures and Skill Building

Do you spend a lot of time in your living room?

Yes, I spend a lot of time in the/my living room.

No, I don't spend a lot of time in/the/my living room.

Does your family spend a lot of time in the living room?

Yes, my family spends (they spend) a lot of time in the living room.

Is there a TV in the living room?

Yes, there's a TV in the living room.

No, there isn't (there's not) a TV in the living room.

Where do you usually sit to watch TV?

I usually sit in the/on the _____.

What is your favorite piece of furniture in the living room? Why?

My favorite piece of furniture in the living room is the/a/an _____ because (reason)/I like it because_____.

Is there a fireplace in the living room?

Yes, there is a fireplace in the living room.

No, there isn't a fireplace in the living room.

Do you have lamps or ceiling lights in the living room?

We have _____ in the living room.

Who builds the fire in your fireplace?

My (name of person) _____ builds the fire.

We never have a fire in the fireplace.

Do you have a separate dining room or just a dining area.

We have a separate dining room/a dining area?

Do you eat in the dining room/dining area every day or only on special occasions?

We eat in the dining room/dining area every day.

We eat in the dining room/dining area only on special occasions.

For what occasions do you use the dining room/dining area?

We use the dining room/dining area for/when/during _____.

When you have company, where do you eat?

When we have company, we eat in the _____.

Do you use the "good" china, silver, and crystal when you have company?

Yes, we use the good china, silver, and crystal when we have company.

No, we don't use the good china, silver, and crystal when we have company.

Do you have an entry hall in your house/apartment?

Yes, I/we do have an entry hall in my/our house/apartment.

No, we don't have an entry hall in my/our house/apartment.

Is there any furniture in the entry hall?

Yes, there is furniture in the entry hall.

No, there isn't any furniture in the entry hall.

What kind of furniture?

There are _____ and _____ .

Are there other halls in your house (corridors in your building)?

Yes, there are other halls in my/our house/corridors in my/our building.

No, there aren't other halls in my/our house/corridors in my/our building.

Using drawing of floor plan: Show us how the hall connects the rooms. Tell us how you pass from one room to another.

31

Rooms in the Home II

The Kitchen

Competency Goals

To be able to give information about yourself and seek information from others with regard to the kitchen and objects found therein.

To be able to identify objects commonly found in kitchens.

To be able to draw a basic floor plan of your kitchen showing the position of all your appliances.

Vocabulary: Listen, Read, Say

stove / stove top (gas / electric)	pots
burners / burner protective insert	pans
hood / fan	skillet / frying pan
oven / convection oven	Dutch oven
microwave / microwave oven	
tea kettle	appliances
broiler	toaster / toaster oven
rack(s)	electric knife
hood	can opener / electric can opener
	food processor
refrigerator	blender
freezer	coffee maker
ice maker	
cabinet(s)	measuring cups
cupboard(s)	measuring spoons
shelf / shelves	funnel
sink / faucet	canisters
garbage disposal	dishwasher

trash compacter	dishwashing detergent/liquid
counter	dish towel
cutting board	sponge
drawers	
garbage can	gadgets
center butcher block table	
	clock
table	window
chairs	curtains/blinds/shades/shutters
place setting: dishes, glassware, silverware, etc.	floor: tile, hardwood, linoleum, etc.
salt and pepper shakers	telephone
napkins	
napkin holder	paper towels
placemats	paper towel holder

Structures and Skill Building

Do you have a big kitchen or a small kitchen?

I/We have a (size) kitchen.

Do you have an eating area in your kitchen? Describe it. If you don't have an eating area in your kitchen, where do you eat?

Yes, I/We have an eating area in my/our kitchen. It's (explain).

No, I/we don't have an eating area in my/our kitchen. I/We eat (explain).

What shape and size is your table?

My/Our table is (explain).

Do you have a lot of *gadgets* in your kitchen? What are some of them?

Yes, I/we have a lot of gadgets in our kitchen. I/We have a/an _____, _____, and _____.

No I/we don't have a lot of gadgets in my/our kitchen.

Who does most of the cooking in your kitchen?

My (name of person) does most of the cooking in my/our kitchen.

Using the drawing of your floor plan:

Show us the floor plan of your kitchen.

Explain your floor plan by telling where all the appliances are.

Where is the eating area?

32

Rooms in the Home III

The Bedroom

Competency Goals

To be able to give information about yourself and seek information from others with regard to the bedroom and objects found therein.

To be able to identify objects commonly found in bedrooms.

To be able to draw a basic floor plan of your own bedroom, showing the position of the furniture.

Vocabulary: Listen, Read, Say

bed	night stand
twin	
double	lamp
queen	lampshade
king	night light
California king	
water bed	bureau
	dresser
headboard	chest of drawers
footboard	drawers
spring(s)	
mattress and box spring	dressing table/vanity
mattress cover	bench/stool
mattress pad	mirror
pillow	closet (standard/walk-in)
regular	shelf/shelves
king size	

pillowcase	window
	curtains / shades / shutters
sheet	
blanket	rug / carpet
comforter	
quilt	chair
bedspread	TV
bed ruffle	
"bed in a bag"	alarm clock
	radio
trundle bed / chest bed	clock radio
bunk / bunk beds	pictures
hide-a-way bed	
roll-a-way bed	to share a bedroom
sofa bed	
cot	to make a bed
sleeping bag	to take care of
	to be comfortable
nursery	to sleep
changing table	to take a nap
crib / bassinet	to rest
mobile	to lie down
rocking chair	
bedside table	
night table	

Structures and Skill Building

How many bedrooms are there in your home/dwelling?

There are (number) bedrooms in my/our home/apartment.

Who shares the bedrooms?

My (name of person) and (name of person), etc. share a bedroom.

No one shares a bedroom.

Do all the beds get made every day?

Yes, all beds get made every day.

No, all beds don't get made every day.

Who makes the beds every day?

Everyone makes their own bed every day.

My mother makes all beds every day.

(Name of person) makes the beds every day.

Who takes care of your bedroom?

I take care of my bedroom.

My sister/brother takes care of my/our bedroom.

My sister/brother and I take care of my/our bedroom.

What do you do to keep your bedroom clean and neat?

I (explain).

What size bed do you sleep in?

I sleep in a (size bed).

Is your bedroom large or small?

My bedroom is (size).

Is it comfortable?

Yes, it is comfortable.

No, it isn't comfortable.

33

Rooms in the Home IV

The Bathroom

Competency Goals

To be able to give information about yourself and seek information from others with regard to bathroom facilities in your home.

To be able to draw a basic floor plan of your bathroom(s) showing where all the objects are.

To be able to identify objects commonly found in bathrooms.

Vocabulary: Listen, Read, Say

bathroom	Kleenex/tissue
guest bathroom	Kleenex/tissue box
	Kleenex/tissue dispenser
bathtub/tub	
shower	medicine chest/cabinet
shower curtain	cabinet(s)
shower stall	shelf/shelves
hot water faucet	mirror
cold water faucet	
shower head	clothes hamper
drain	laundry hamper
drain plug	
body soap	rug
shampoo/conditioner	
	bathroom scale
tile	
bathmat	ventilator/fan
	electrical outlet(s)

toilet	
toilet bowl	towel
toilet seat	bath towel (jumbo)
toilet seat cover	face towel
handle	fingertip towel
to flush	wash cloth
toilet paper	towel rack
toilet paper dispenser	hook
sink	to wash
hand soap / soap dish	to bathe / to shower
soap dispenser	to turn the water off / on
toothbrush / electric toothbrush	to weigh yourself
toothpaste	
water pick	sponge
dental floss	back scrubber (brush)
mouthwash	"scrubby"
electric razor	
razor	
razor blades	
shaving cream	

Structures and Skill Building

How many bathrooms are there in your house/apartment?

There is/are (amount) bathroom/bathrooms in my house/apartment.

What floor is it on?

It's on the _____ floor.

Are they all/both on the same floor?

Yes, they're on the _____ floor.

No, one's on the _____ floor and the other's on the _____ floor.

Is the shower in the bathtub or in a separate shower stall?

The shower is in the bathtub/a separate shower stall.

Do you prefer to take showers or baths?

I prefer to take showers/baths.

How often do you take a shower/bath?

I take a shower/bath (amount).

How often do you weigh yourself?

I weigh myself (amount).

34

Household Chores and Home Maintenance

Competency Goals

To be able to give information about yourself and seek information from others with regard to household chores and maintenance.

To be able to identify various household appliances and how they are used.

Vocabulary: Listen, Read, Say

to maintain	to replace
to repair/fix	
	to do the grocery shopping
to clean	to prepare the menus
to wash	to set the table
to scrub	
to dry	to be responsible for
	to get an allowance
to change	to get paid for
to sweep	
to mop	washing machine
to shine/polish	dryer
	laundromat (coin operated)
to dust	
to vacuum	iron
	ironing board
to empty	starch
to take out	steam

to mow/cut	vacuum cleaner
to rake	vacuum bag
to week	attachments
to trim	
to edge	mop
	broom/electric broom
to paint	dustpan
to babysit	scrub brush
	sponge
to animal sit	dust cloth/rag
to feed (pets)	furniture polish
to walk	window/glass cleaner
to clean the cage, crate	wax
to do the dishes (wash and dry)	disinfectants
to load the dishwasher	cleanser
to unload the dishwasher	Clorox wipes
	bucket/pail
to do the laundry	
to go to the laundromat	dishwasher
to iron	garbage disposal
to fold	trash compacter
to wash	cord/extension cord
to put away	electrical outlet

Structures and Skill Building

Do you have chores at home?

Yes, I have chores at home.

No, I don't have any chores at home.

What are your chores each day?

I (explain).

I have to (explain).

What are your chores on the weekend?

I (explain).

I have to (explain).

Do you have any pets? What kind?

Yes, I have a (type(s).

No, I don't have any pets.

Who takes care of your pet(s)?

(Person) takes care of my pet(s).

What has to be done? (Explanation)

Who does the grocery shopping? How often?

(Person) does the grocery shopping. (Amount)

Who cooks/prepares the meals at your house/apartment?

(Person) cooks the meals at my/our house/apartment.

Who clears the table at your house/apartment?

(Person) clears the table at my/our house/apartment.

Who does the laundry at your house/apartment?

(Person(s) does/do the laundry at my/our house/apartment.

Do you have a washing machine and dryer or do you go to the laundromat?

I (explanation).

Who irons?

(Person(s)) iron/irons.

Who dusts?

(Person(s)) dust/dusts.

What kind of furniture polish do you use?

(Person(s)) use/uses (brand name).

What kind of glass cleaner do you use?

(Person(s)) use/uses (brand name).

Who vacuums?

(Person(s)) vacuum/vacuums.

Who cleans the bathroom(s)?

(Person(s))clean/cleans the bathroom(s).

Who empties/takes out the garbage?

(Person(s)) empty/empties the garbage.

Who fixes/repairs things when they break?

(Person(s))fix/fixes things that break.

What are some other chores done regularly at your house/apartment?

(Explain). (Person(s)) do/does (chore/chores).

Do you get an allowance for doing chores?

Yes, I get an allowance for doing chores.

No, I don't get an allowance for doing chores.

How much do you get? How often?

I get (amount) (when).

Who does the yard work/takes care of the yard at your house/apartment?

(Person(s)) do/does the yard work/takes care of the yard at my/our house/apartment.

35

The Post Office

Competency Goals

To be able to give information about yourself and seek information from others with regard to transactions at the post office.

To be able to address envelopes correctly.

To have a general knowledge of the U.S. Postal System.

Vocabulary: Listen, Read, Say

to send	mail
to mail	mail truck
to register	mailbag
to certify	letter
to deliver	envelope(s)
	self-sealing envelopes
to weigh	bubble envelope
to insure	stamps
to collect (stamps)	roll of stamps
to lose (a package/letter)	airmail stamp
to return/send back	airmail
to wait on	special delivery
to look for	priority mail (overnight, next day mail)
to arrive	commemorative stamp
to pay	stamp machine
to write	
	stamp collection
home delivery	to have a stamp collection

general delivery	return to sender
COD (collect on delivery)	mailbox
postal clerk	letter slot
postal service	regular mail
clerk's window	first class mail
	registered mail
UPS (United Parcel Service)	
Fed Ex (Federal Express)	scale
post office	ounce (28.4 grams)
postman/letter carrier/postal carrier/mail carrier	pound (16 ounces)
postage	package
insurance	zip code
domestic postage	money order
foreign postage	postcard
address/return address	to wire money
postmark	
PO Box (post office box)	U.S. Postal Service online/website

Structures and Skill Building

Have you ever gone to the post office?

Yes, I have.

No, I haven't.

Where is the nearest post office from your home?

The nearest post office is _____.

Why did you go to the post office?

I went because _____.

I went to _____.

Do you ever write to friends and relatives in your native country? Who?

Yes, I write to _____.

No, I don't write to anyone in my native country.

How much does it cost to mail a letter to someone in your native country?

It costs _____ to mail a letter to someone in my native country.

How much does a stamp cost for a regular letter in the United States?

A stamp costs _____ for a regular letter in the United States.

How much does a stamp cost for a special delivery letter in the United States?

A stamp costs _____ for a special delivery letter in the United States.

How much does it cost to mail a postcard?

It costs _____ to mail a postcard.

Do you have a pen pal? Where? Who?

Yes, I have a pen pal in _____. His/Her name is _____.

No I don't have a pen pal.

Do you collect stamps?

Yes, I collect stamps.

No, I don't collect stamps.

Do you know anyone/anybody who collects stamps? Who?

Yes, _____ collects stamps.

No, I don't know anyone/anybody who collects stamps.

36

Time, the Calendar, Holidays, and Celebrations

Competency Goals

To be able to give information about yourself and seek information from others with regard to time, the calendar, holidays, birthdays, school events, and the like.

To be able to fill out a blank calendar by writing in the days, dates, holidays, birthdays, school events, and the like.

To understand the U.S. time zones.

To know the holidays that are celebrated in the United States.

To be familiar with the horoscope.

Vocabulary: Listen, Read, Say

Time

year	o'clock (of the clock)
leap year	a.m. (ante meridian)
school year	p.m. (post meridian)
midnight	clock/watch/wristwatch/cell phone
noon	face
morning	hands: minute/hour/second
afternoon	digital
evening	solar
dusk	stopwatch
twilight	clock radio
dawn	alarm clock
daylight	cuckoo clock
standard time	grandfather clock

daylight savings time	
	yesterday (past)
weekday	today (present)
weekend	tomorrow (future)
long weekend	
	time zones: Pacific/Rocky Mountain/Central/ Eastern
decade	
century	school day
millennium	school night
time	Monday
second	Tuesday
minute	Wednesday
hour	Thursday
	Friday
hourly	Saturday
daily	Sunday
weekly	
biweekly	
monthly	
bimonthly	
yearly/annually	
daytime	
nighttime	

The Calendar

to be born/to die (deceased)	May
day/date	June
month/day/year	July
week of	August
	September
January	October

February	November
March	December
April	

The Astrological Calendar

Astrological calendar begins with Aries	Leo: July 23 to August 21
your horoscope sign/your sign	Virgo: August 22 to September 23
signs of the Zodiac	Libra: September 24 to October 23
	Scorpio: October 24 to November 22
Aries: March 21 to April 20	Sagittarius: November 23 to December 22
Taurus: April 21 to May 21	Capricorn: December 23 to January 20
Gemini: May 22 to June 21	Aquarius: January 21 to February 19
Cancer: June 22 to July 22	Pisces: February 20 to March 20

U.S. Holidays and Celebrations

January	New Year's Day
	Martin Luther King, Jr.'s birthday
February	Chinese New Year
	Abraham Lincoln's birthday
	George Washington's birthday/Presidents' Day
	Valentine's Day
	Groundhog Day
March	St. Patrick's Day
	Easter (late March)
April	Easter (early April)
	April Fools' Day (All Fools' Day)
May	May Day
	Cinco de Mayo
	Mother's Day
	Memorial Day

June	Flag Day
	Father's Day
July	Independence Day / Fourth of July
August	
September	Labor Day
	Yom Kippur
	Rosh Hashanah
October	Columbus Day / Indigenous People's Day
	Halloween
November	Veteran's Day
	Thanksgiving Day
December	Christmas Day
	Chanukah
	New Year's Eve

Structures and Skill Building

What time is it?

It's _____.

What's the date today?

What's the date?

What's today's date?

Today is _____.

It's _____.

What was yesterday's date?

Yesterday's date was _____.

It was _____.

What will be tomorrow's date?

What will the date be tomorrow?

Tomorrow's date will be _____.

It will be _____.

What is the date of your birthday?

When's your birthday?

My birthdate is (It's) _____.

My birthday is (It's) _____.

When were you born?

I was born on _____.

What day was it?

It was a _____.

What's your sign?

My sign is (it's) _____.

What does it mean?

It means (explanation).

I don't know what it means.

What time do you usually get up on school days?

I usually get up at _____ on school days.

What time do you usually go to bed on school nights?

I usually go to bed at _____.

What time do you usually get up on the weekend?

I usually get up at _____ on the weekend.

What time do you usually go to bed on Friday and Saturday night?

I usually go to bed at _____ on Friday and Saturday night.

What time do you usually get up during summer vacation?

I usually get up at _____ during summer vacation.

What time do you usually go to bed during summer vacation?

I usually go to bed at _____ during summer vacation.

What's your favorite day? Why?

My favorite day is _____ because _____.

What is your favorite month? Why?

My favorite month is _____ because _____.

When does your family usually (take a/go on a) vacation?

My family usually (takes a/goes on a) vacation in/during _____.

What is your favorite American holiday? Why?

My favorite holiday in America is _____because _____.

What are some of the holidays you celebrated in your native country? When/In what month did they fall/occur?

We celebrated _____ in _____ and _____ in _____.

Do you still celebrate any of your native holidays now that you're living in America? Which one(s)? When?

Yes, we still celebrate _____ in/during _____.

No, we don't celebrate any of our native holidays.

Explain how you celebrated (name of holiday) in (name of native country).

How do you celebrate (name of holiday) here in America?

37

Weather and Seasons

Competency Goals

To be able to give information about yourself and seek information from others with regard to weather and seasons.

To be able to understand a weather forecast by reading about it in the newspaper, reading about it online, watching television, and listening to the radio.

To be able to understand and define the words Fahrenheit, centigrade, and Celsius.

Vocabulary: Listen, Read, Say

cloudy (overcast)/clouds	normal
rainy/rain/raindrops/rainfall/sprinkling/ pouring/downpour	above/below normal
snowing/snow/snowflakes/snowstorm/ snowman	
hail/hailstorm/hailing	to predict
sunny/sun/sunshine	to freeze
foggy/fog	to melt
smoggy/smog	to perspire
hazy/haze	to cloud up/over
windy/wind/windstorm	to storm
	thunder and lightening
climate	
weather	weatherman/weathergirl
temperature	weather patterns
tropics/tropical	prediction/forecast
arctic	satellite weather forecast
seasonal	Doppler radar

hot	degree/degrees
warm	zero
cold	Fahrenheit
cool	centigrade
dry	Celsius
damp/humid	
humidity	barometer
freezing	pressure (rising and falling)
	barometric pressure
good	
bad	spring
fair	summer
	autumn/fall
hurricane	
tornado	
typhoon	
monsoon	
flood/flash flood warnings	
tidal wave	
tsunami	
ice/icicles	
draught	

Structures and Skill Building

What's the weather like today?

What's it like (out/outside) today?

It's _____ today.

It's (very/awful/a little) _____ today.

What did the weatherman/weathergirl predict/forecast for today?

The weatherman/weathergirl (predicted/forecast) _____ for today.

What was the weather like yesterday?

It was _____ yesterday.

It was (awfully/very/a little) _____ yesterday.

What do you predict/forecast the weather will be (like) tomorrow?

I (predict/forecast) the weather/it will be _____ tomorrow.

What season are we in?

What season is it?

We're in _____.

It's _____.

What is the weather usually like here during (name of season)?

The weather is/It's usually _____ during (name of season).

What is the weather usually like in your country during (name of season)?

The weather is/It's usually _____ during (name of season).

Did you ever have any terrible storms in your country? What kind?

Yes, we had (type of storm).

No, we never had any terrible storms.

Have you ever been in a tornado, hurricane, or monsoon? Describe it.

Yes, I've been in a (name). It was (describe).

No, I've never been in a tornado, hurricane, or monsoon.

What clothing do you usually wear in/during the winter/summer?

I usually wear (clothing) during/in (name of season).

38

Transportation I

By Road

Competency Goals

To be able to give information about yourself and seek information from others with regard to the car, car transportation, and maintenance.

To be able to identify specific parts on a car.

To be able to name and identify common street and road signs.

To understand the consequences of *unsafe driving* (traffic tickets, high insurance costs, etc.).

Vocabulary: Listen, Read, Say

to drive	highway patrol
to start	traffic ticket/citation
to stop	moving violation
to yield	nonmoving violation
to travel	parking ticket
to park	traffic court
to parallel park	traffic school
to blow the horn	ticket/violation fees/court fees
to honk the horn	car insurance
to work	high risk insurance
to function	driving record
to turn on/off	
to turn right/left	mirror
to have a flat (flat tire)	rearview mirror
	window
automobile/auto/car/electric car/hybrid car	side mirrors
used car	sun visor

new car	armrest
engine/motor	hardtop/convertible
driver/motorist	door
interior	door handle
front seat	door locks
back seat/rear seat	starter/key/push button starter
bucket seats/bench seat	battery
infant car seat	clutch
children's/toddler's car seat	accelerator/gas pedal/pedal
seat belt	tires (flat/spare)
	jack
steering wheel/wheel	bumper
horn	rims (chrome/mags/spokes)
turn signals/hand signals	gas tank
emergency lights	
windshield	make and model of car
windshield wipers	names of cars
defroster/air/air conditioner/heater	rebuilt or stock
hood	
glove box/compartment	carwash
center glove box/compartment	gas station
dashboard	service station
radio/CD player/GPS/screen/Bluetooth/ screen menu	to pump gas
air bag/air bags	to get gas
clock	to service
vent/vents	to check the oil/to check the fluids
	to check the tires, battery, etc.
driver's permit	to change a flat/flat tire
driver's manual	
driver's test: written and *behind the wheel* tests	types of gas: regular/leaded/unleaded/super unleaded/diesel
driver's license	antifreeze
eye chart test	
	stop light

license plate	red light
personalized license plate	yellow light
bumper sticker(s)	green light
	blinking lights
transmission	
standard / manual / stick shift / automatic	to rent a car
odometer	compact / economy / mid-size / standard / luxury / SUV (sports utility vehicle)
tachometer (tach)	unlimited mileage
speed / speedometer	valid driver's license
speed limit	limousine / limo
mph (miles per hour)	rental car contract
stop sign / signal / arterial	
freeway	
highway	electronic fast pass (for bridge tolls)
expressway	
overpass	
diamond lane / commute lane	

Structures and Skill Building

Does anyone in your family own a car? Who?

Yes, my _____ owns a car.

No, no one in my family owns a car.

What kind of car?

It's a/an _____.

Who drives the car?

My _____ and _____ drive the car.

Where is the car serviced?

The/Our car is serviced at _____.

What kind of gas does the car use?

The car uses _____ gas.

Does your car have air conditioning?

Yes, our/my car has air conditioning?

No, our/my car does not have air conditioning.

Have you ever been though a carwash?

Yes, I have/I've been through a carwash. It felt (explain).

No, I haven't ever been through a carwash.

Do you ever wash the car yourself?

Yes, I sometimes wash the car myself.

No, I don't ever wash the car myself.

What does a red light mean?

A red light means STOP.

What does a yellow light mean?

A yellow light means CAUTION/YIELD.

What does a green light mean?

A green light means GO.

What kind of car do you want to have when you grow up/someday?

I want to have a/an _____ when I grow up/someday.

Has anyone in your family ever rented a car? When? From which company?

Yes, we/my _____ rented a car (explain). It was from (name of company).

How much does it cost to rent a car? Per day? Per week?

39

Transportation II

Public Transportation

Competency Goals

To be able to give information about yourself and seek information from others with regard to public transportation.

To know who to call and what to ask for with regard to information about transportation schedules and times.

Vocabulary: Listen, Read, Say

General Terminology

public transportation	to pay
mass transit	
local	corner
commuter	center island / divider
long distance	destination
transcontinental	schedule(s)
	station
to take	stops / scheduled stops
to catch	
to buy	

Bus

local	bus driver
transit	fare / token
transcontinental	bus line #
bus station	transfer
bus stop	route
bus driver	pass / bus pass

124

Street Car/Trolley

street car line / trolley line	street car / trolley line
fare / token	transfer
stop / stops	

Taxi/Cab

taxi cab / taxi / cab	tip
taxi cab driver / cab driver	UBER (personal car driver; cell phone app)
meter	rates
fare	

Cable Car

cable car barn	bell
fare	cable car line #
stop / stops	transfer
brakeman	turntable

Subway/Rapid Transit System

subway / subway station	ticket / token (single trip / round trip)
turnstile	platform

Limousine

driver / chauffeur	to rent
uniform	to hire
fare	

Structures and Skill Building

Do you ever take the bus around (your city)?

Yes, I sometimes take the bus around (your city)?

No, I never take the bus around (your city).

Have you ever taken the bus to get out of (your city)? Where did you go?

Yes, I've taken the bus to _____.

No, I've never taken the bus to get out of (your city).

How would you find out the schedule of a certain bus in (your city)?

I'd (explain).

How would you get from (your city) to (another city)?

I'd (explain).

Have you ever taken a cab/taxi?

Yes, I've taken a cab/taxi.

No, I've never/I haven't taken a cab/taxi.

Have you ever ridden on a subway? Where?

Yes, I've ridden on a subway in _____.

No, I haven't/I've never ridden on a subway.

Have you ever ridden on a street car/trolley car? Where?

Yes, I've ridden on a trolley car/street car in _____.

No, I haven't/I've never ridden on a trolley car/street car.

Have you ever seen a limousine?

Yes, I've seen a limousine.

No, I've never/I haven't seen a limousine.

Who usually rides in limousines?

Famous people usually ride in limousines.

Why are many high school students renting limousines on prom nights?

Many high school students are renting limousines on prom night because _____.

Calling a Cab/Taxi

(Name of Cab Company). May I help you?

Yes, please. I'd like a cab/taxi sent to (give address and city) as soon as possible.

And where are you going? And what is your destination?

(Give destination.)

We'll get a cab/taxi/one right out to you. It will be about _____ minutes.

Thank you. Good-bye.

Good-bye.

40

Transportation III

Alternatives by Road

Competency Goals

To be able to give information about yourself and seek information from others with regard to alternative modes of transportation by road.

To be able to give directions (verbally and in writing) on how to get from one place to another.

To be able to follow directions (verbally and in writing) on how to get from one place to another.

To be able to read a map and understand the GPS system.

Vocabulary: Listen, Read, Say

Truck

transporter	van
semi	truck and trailer
pickup	18-wheeler
cab	10-wheeler (truck with bed)

Motorcycle

helmet	exhaust pipe/exhaust
facemask/shield	starter
rear light	gearshift
seat	clutch
accelerator	gas tank
brake	radio
saddlebag	GPS system

Motor Scooter

vespa	moped
scooter	helmet

Bicycle

helmet	spokes
mirror	valves
cable(s)	brakes
headlight	pedal
reflector(s)	chain
handlebars	sprocket
seat	bicycle pump
basket	kickstand
wheel(s)	bearings
tire(s)	

Related Terminology

camper/mobile home	giving directions
skateboard/hoverboard	asking for directions
disadvantages	
advantages	by/on foot

Structures and Skill Building

Do you like to walk?

Yes, I do like to walk.

No, I don't like to walk.

Do you walk a lot?

Yes, I do walk a lot.

No, I don't walk a lot.

Do you walk to school?

Yes, I do walk to school.

No, I don't walk to school.

What are some types of trucks? What are they used for?

There's a/the _____. It's used for _____. There's a/the _____. It's used for _____.

Have you ever ridden in a truck? If so, what kind?

Yes, I've ridden in a/an _____ truck.

Whose truck was it?

It was my _____'s truck.

Do you know anyone who owns a motorcycle? Who?

No, I don't know anyone who owns a motorcycle.

Yes, I know someone who owns a motorcycle. He's/She's my _____.

His/Her name is _____.

What kind of motorcycle does he/she have?

He/She has a/an _____.

Have you ever ridden on his/her motorcycle?

Yes, I've ridden on his/her motorcycle.

No, I've never ridden on a motorcycle.

What are some advantages of a motorcycle?

One advantage of a motorcycle is _____. Another is _____.

What are some disadvantages of a motorcycle?

One disadvantage of a motorcycle is _____. Another is _____.

Do you know anyone who owns a motor scooter? Who?

Yes, I know someone who owns a motor scooter. He's/She's my _____. His/Her name is _____.

Have you ever ridden on a hoverboard?

Yes, I've ridden on a hoverboard.

No, I haven't ridden on a hoverboard.

41

Transportation IV
The Train

Competency Goals

To be able to give information about yourself and seek information from others with regard to transportation by train.

To be able to purchase a train ticket.

To know how to read a train timetable.

Vocabulary: Listen, Read, Say

to take (a train)	railroad station
to catch (a train)	train station
to travel	train
to buy (a ticket)	freight train
to depart/leave	passenger train
to arrive	express train
to take a trip by train	commuter train
to stop (a)/to make a stop	transcontinental train
to eat/dine in the dining car/diner	locomotive
	engine
ticket window	engineer
ticket	conductor
one-way ticket	porter
round-trip ticket	caboose
online ticket	brakeman
	signalman
schedule	signal box
timetable	signal(s)
	whistle

baggage/luggage	
briefcase/carry on (luggage)	platform/platform number
baggage check/claim	track/tracks
suitcase/bag	ties
luggage rack	switch
passenger(s)	buffer
compartment	flag
first class	diesel
second class	electric
coach	late
Pullman/sleeping car	early
snack bar	on time
club car	All aboard!
seat	

Structures and Skill Building

Have you ever ridden on a train?

Yes, I've ridden on a train.

No, I've never ridden/I haven't ever ridden on a train.

If your answer was yes, was it a commuter train (local train) or a transcontinental (long distance) train?

It was a _____ train.

From where (what station) did you leave?

We/I left from (city) or the _____ station in (city).

Where did you go?

We/I went to (city).

Did you eat on the train?

Yes, we/I ate on the train.

No, we/I didn't eat on the train.

If your answer was yes, did you bring your own food to eat in the dining car or snack bar?

We/I (explain).

Was there a dining car or just a snack bar?

There was a (explain).

Was there a club car?

Yes, there was a club car.

No, there wasn't a club car.

Did the train make many stops?

Yes, the train (it) made many stops.

No, the train (it) didn't make many stops.

If your answer was yes, did you ever get off the train when it stopped and browse around the station?

Yes, I got off the train when it stopped and browsed around the station.

No, I didn't get off the train when it stopped.

Did you sleep on the train?

Yes, I slept on the train.

No, I didn't sleep on the train.

If your answer was yes, did you sleep in your seat or in a sleeping car/Pullman?

I slept _____.

Did you enjoy your trip?

Yes, I enjoyed my trip.

No, I didn't enjoy my trip.

Are there trains in your native country?

Yes, there are trains in my native country.

No, there aren't any trains in my native country.

If your answer was yes, did you ever ride the train in your native country?

Yes, I did ride/rode the train in my native country.

No, I didn't ride the train in my native country.

42

Transportation V

By Air

Competency Goals

To be able to give information about yourself and seek information from others with regard to transportation by air.

To become familiar with airline terminology.

To be able to make an airline reservation over the phone and online.

Vocabulary: Listen, Read, Say

to make a reservation	cockpit
to reserve a seat	engine
to be confirmed / confirmation number	instrument panel
to check in	wing
to check in (luggage)	tail
to board	wheel
to be arriving / arrivals	landing gear
to be departing / leaving / departures	cabin
	seat
airport / airport terminal	
airplane	propeller
pilot / co-pilot	prop plane
captain / co-captain	jet
flight attendant / steward / stewardess	travel agent
passenger	travel agency
flight / flight number	credit card
ticket / online ticket	expiration date / security numbers on back
reservation	confirmation

first class	
economy / coach class	seat assignment: aisle or window seat
fare / price	takeoff / departure
control tower	landing / arrival
air traffic controller	on time
runway	canceled
hanger(s)	delayed
ticket counter	
reservation desk / counter	domestic flights
gate	international flights
boarding pass	
carry-on luggage / baggage / bag / suitcase	hijack / hijackers
baggage claim area	hostages
baggage check	demands / ransom(s)
customs	
immigration	round trip
passport / visa	one way
	open return
Transportation Security Administration (TSA) / airport security	stop over
no return / no exit	direct flight / nonstop flight
	seatbelt
air sickness / air sickness bag	earphones
oxygen mask	in-flight Wi-Fi
emergency information	
emergency exit(s)	to turn off all electronic devices
seat cushions	onboard movie
flotation device / vest	beverage service
	meal
kiosk	snack

Structures and Skill Building

Have you ever ridden in an airplane?

Yes, I have / I've ridden in an airplane.

No, I haven't ridden in an airplane.

From where did you take off?

We/I took off from _____.

Where did you land?

We/I landed in _____.

Do you know anyone who owns his/her own plane? Who?

Yes, (person) owns his/her own plane.

Yes, I know someone who owns his/her own plane. He's/She's/It's my _____.

No, I don't know anyone/anybody who owns his/her own plane.

What are some uses of helicopters?

Helicopters are used for traffic patrol, rescue missions, taking people to the airport, or taking people to a job site.

Do you know anyone who flies a helicopter? Who?

Yes, (person) flies a helicopter.

Yes, I know someone who flies a helicopter. He's/She's/It's my _____.

No, I don't know anyone/anybody who flies a helicopter.

Making an Airplane Reservation: By Phone

Hello, United Airlines flight information and reservations. May I help you?

Yes, I'd like to make a reservation on an early morning flight to New Orleans, Louisiana, on Thursday, May 3.

Where (What airport) will you be departing from?

San Francisco International Airport.

One moment, please while I check the flights. We have a 5:00 a.m. flight arriving at New Orleans at 4:30 p.m.

I'd like the 5:00 a.m. flight please.

Do you wish a return flight? Do you wish to make reservations on a return flight?

Yes, mid-morning on Wednesday, May 4.

We have a flight leaving/departing New Orleans at 9:30 a.m. and arriving in San Francisco at 4:00 p.m.

I'd like the 9:30 a.m. flight, please.

OK. You're confirmed on Flight 709 leaving San Francisco on Tuesday, May 3, at 5:00 a.m. arriving at New Orleans at 4:30 p.m. Return Flight 57 leaving/departing New Orleans on Wednesday, May 4, at 9:30 a.m. arriving at San Francisco at 4:00.

Round trip fare is $800.00. How would you like to pay for the tickets? How do you wish to pay for the tickets?

I'll pay with my Visa credit card.

May I have your last name please?

O'SULLIVAN

First name?

BRITTANY

Middle initial?

J.

Home phone?

555-516-7575

Business phone?

555-516-2212

And may I have your Visa number, expiration date, and security code on the back of your card?

1234 5678 9999. The expiration date is July 2020 and the security code is 987.

Thank you for calling United Airlines. Hope you enjoy your flight.

Thank you and good-bye.

At the Airport Ticket Counter

Good morning. Where will you be traveling today? May I see your ID, tickets, and boarding pass, please?

We are traveling to New Orleans, Louisiana. (Hand the attendant your ID, ticket, and boarding pass.)

And do you have any luggage/bags to check in? How many will you be checking?

Just one. (Put your bag on the luggage scale.)

Thank you. (The attendant returns your ID/ticket and boarding pass and claim stub for your luggage.) Your flight will be departing from Gate 47, but first you will need to go through the security checkpoint right over there.

Thank you.

At the Gate

Good morning. May I see your ID, ticket, and boarding pass, please?

You are all set to go. Your seat assignment is on your ticket.

Have a pleasant flight.

43

Transportation VI

By Water

Competency Goals

To be able to give information about yourself and seek information from others with regard to transportation by water.

To be able to identify specific modes of transportation (sailboat, rowboat, motorboat, jet ski, etc.) and how they are used.

Vocabulary: Listen, Read, Say

General Terminology

to leave/depart	ship/boat
to dock	smokestack
to take a voyage	anchor
to go on a cruise	buoy
to sail	cable
to row	forklift
to paddle	horizon
to steer	port
to cruise	starboard
	bow
pier	midship
gangway	stern
warehouse	
crane	deck
wharf	harbor/port
cargo	starboard/port

Sailboat

sail	rudder
mast	keel

Motorboat

outboard motor	inboard motor

Cruise Ship/Ocean Liner

captain	dining room
crew	swimming pool
porthole	bar/lounge
stateroom	gym/spa/sauna
cabin	hot tub
life boats/life boat drill	tenders/commuter boats or ships

Jet Ski

personal water craft	gear(s)
throttle	life vest—mandatory

Rowboat

oars	oar lock

Canoe

paddle(s)	

Ferryboat

on deck	in the lounge

Emergency Equipment/Services

life vest/jacket	flares
life preserver	lifeboats
flare guns	life rafts

U.S. Coast Guard	
Sheriff's Department	
Police Department	

Other Forms of Water Transportation

tugboat	trawler
freighter	tanker
barge	

Structures and Skill Building

Have you ever traveled by ship? How old were you?

Yes, I traveled by ship when I was _____ years old.

No, I've never traveled by ship.

If your answer was yes, from which port did you depart/leave?

I/We departed/left from the port of _____.

At which port did you dock?

I/We docked at the port of _____.

Describe the ship. Was it big, small, new, old, comfortable?

The ship/It was (explain).

Have you ever traveled by water?

Yes, I have traveled by water.

No, I've never traveled by water.

If your answer was yes, what mode of water transportation did you use?

I/We (explain).

Have you ever been sailing?

Yes, I've been sailing.

No, I haven't been sailing.

44

Taking a Vacation/Trip

Competency Goals

To be able to give information about yourself and seek information from others with regard to vacations and trips.

To be able to give an oral and written report about your favorite vacation, your worst vacation and your dream vacation.

Vocabulary: Listen, Read, Say

to plan a vacation/trip	maid service
to take a vacation/trip	bellhop
to go on a vacation/trip	hotel/motel amenities
to make a reservation on a/an/the (mode of transportation)	tip/gratuity
to go by plane/train/bus/ship/cab	Check out time is _____.
to take a (guided) tour	vacation trip/business trip
to walk (tour)	tour guide
to take a bus/car	tour/tourist
to buy/get travelers' checks	
to send/make a deposit	Do you have any vacancies?
to pay in advance	Vacancy/no vacancies
to take photos/pictures	What's the rate for a single (room)?
to buy/get souvenirs	What's the rate for a double (room)?
	a single room with a twin size bed/double bed/queen size bed/king size bed
to make a room reservation	a double room with two double beds/twin size beds/queen size beds/king size beds
to reserve a room	a double room with a twin size and a king size (etc.) bed

to stay at a hotel/motel/guest house/rooming house/inn/dormitory/bed and breakfast/condo/townhouse (time share plan)	a bed/crib/cot
to stay with friends/relatives	a studio
to check in/to check out	
room service	
Do you accept Visa, Master Card, or American Express?	

Structures and Skill Building

How many trips did you go on this year?

I went on (amount) trips this year.

I didn't go on any trips this year.

If you answered yes, tell us about them. (Explain).

What was the best vacation/trip you can remember? When was it? Describe it.

The best vacation/trip I can remember was (explanation including time).

Does your family ever go on special vacation trips? Where?

Yes, (we go/my family goes) on special vacation trips. We go to _____.

When do you usually take these trips?

We usually take these trips in/at _____.

About the Author

University of San Francisco graduate and author Dr. **Kristine Setting Clark** was a long-time feature writer for the San Francisco 49ers' and Dallas Cowboys' *Gameday* Magazine. A gifted athlete in her own right, physical education teacher, wife, mother, and later, a high school administrator and college professor, Dr. Clark has never let anything stand in the way of her goals; not even a life-threatening bout with Hodgkin's Disease, blindness in both eyes for ten months, and the resulting partial blindness, at age twenty-six. Her passion for life, her incredible optimism, and her drive to live life to the fullest has endeared her to her former students, friends, and to those on whom she's written, including her childhood football idol and close friend, Bob St. Clair of the San Francisco 49ers.

Besides *Undefeated, Untied, and Uninvited: A Documentary of the 1951 University of San Francisco Dons' Football Team*, she has authored nine other books: *Legends of the Hall: 1950s*; *St Clair: I'll Take It Raw: The Life of Former San Francisco 49er and Hall of Fame Member, Bob St. Clair* (foreword by Gino Marchetti); *Lilly: A Cowboy's Story—The Life of Former Dallas Cowboys and Hall of Fame Member, Bob Lilly* (foreword by Roger Staubach); *Tittle: Nothing Comes Easy—The Life of Former Football Great and Hall of Fame Member, Y. A. Tittle* (foreword by Frank Gifford); *The Fire Within: The Life of Former Green Bay Packer and Hall of Fame Member, Jim Taylor* (foreword by Bart Starr); and *Controlled Violence: The Life of Former New York Giant, Washington Redskins, and Hall of Fame Member, Sam Huff* (foreword by Frank Gifford).

Released in July 2014 is her latest book, *The Fighting Donovans: A Family History of World Boxing Champion and Hall of Fame Boxer, Mike Donovan, World Champion Boxing Referee and Boxing Hall of Fame Referee Arthur Donovan, Sr. and former Baltimore Colt Defensive Tackle and Pro Football Hall of Fame Member, Arthur Donovan, Jr.* In the summer of 2016 her book on *Football's Fabulous Fifties: When Men Were Men and the Grass Was Still Real*, will be released by St. Johann's Press.

Her book *Cheating Is Encouraged!* with former Raider wide receiver Mike Siani was released through Skyhorse Publishing (an imprint of W.W. Norton) in September 2015. In December 2015 her memoirs on defeating cancer and blindness were published by Amazon. The book is titled *Death Was Never an Option! A Humorously Serious Story on Defeating Cancer and Blindness.*

Over the years, she has also held a number of book-signing events with the many celebrities from her books at the Pro Football Hall of Fame in Canton, Ohio. She has also been a keynote speaker for many corporate, sports, and educational venues. Clark is also an avid advisory board representative for Mike Ditka's Gridiron Greats Assistance Fund. In November 2014, Clark and the Santa Clara Chamber of Commerce officially kicked off their First Annual Chamber of Commerce/49ers/Gridiron Greats luncheon.

Dr. Clark's personality, close relationships with the subjects of her books, and engaging writing style allow her to reach the subject matter on a deeper level, taking the reader to otherwise unavailable territory: the sometimes humorous, always intriguing backstory of the famous events and players in the world of sports. In addition, her achievements have led to being a guest author on major sports talk radio shows. In February 2014, Clark's first book, *Undefeated Untied and Uninvited* was the subject of an ESPN documentary for Black History Month. The documentary, *The '51 Dons*, and was narrated by Johnny Mathis. She is currently working on a treatment for a documentary on her latest book, *The Fighting Donovans*.

In 1977 Clark was diagnosed with Stage IV Hodgkin's Disease and was given three months to live. She eventually beat the disease after enduring ten months of blindness caused by the grueling chemotherapy treatments. Her latest book, an autobiographical memoir, *Death Was Never An Option! A Humorously Serious Story on Beating Cancer* was released in December 2015.

Dr. Clark resides in Stockton, California, has two grown children and four grandsons. Her oldest grandson, Justin, is the godson of former All-Pro 49er and Hall of Fame member Bob St. Clair.